The
Power
of Love

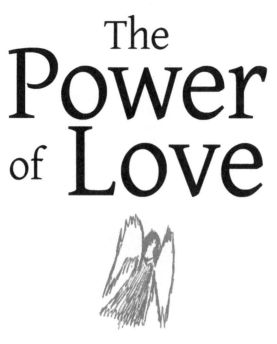

*A Mother's Miraculous Journey from
Grief to Medium, Channel and Teacher*

Heather Scavetta

iUniverse LLC
Bloomington

THE POWER OF LOVE
A MOTHER'S MIRACULOUS JOURNEY FROM GRIEF
TO MEDIUM, CHANNEL AND TEACHER

Scripture quotations are from The Holy Bible, English Standard Version® (ESV®), copyright © 2001 by Crossway, a publishing ministry of Good News Publishers. Used by permission. All rights reserved.

Angel drawing picture provided by Cassandra Scavetta through automatic writing with Elizabeth

Karel Miragaya/123RF cover angel image

iUniverse books may be ordered through booksellers or by contacting:

iUniverse
1663 Liberty Drive
Bloomington, IN 47403
www.iuniverse.com
1-800-Authors (1-800-288-4677)

Because of the dynamic nature of the Internet, any web addresses or links contained in this book may have changed since publication and may no longer be valid. The views expressed in this work are solely those of the author and do not necessarily reflect the views of the publisher, and the publisher hereby disclaims any responsibility for them.

ISBN: 978-1-4917-3565-7 (sc)
ISBN: 978-1-4917-3567-1 (hc)
ISBN: 978-1-4917-3566-4 (e)

Printed in the United States of America.

iUniverse rev. date: 07/31/2014

13 If I speak in the tongues of men and of angels, but have not love, I am a noisy gong or a clanging cymbal. 2 And if I have prophetic powers, and understand all mysteries and all knowledge, and if I have all faith, so as to remove mountains, but have not love, I am nothing. 3 If I give away all I have, and if I deliver up my body to be burned, but have not love, I gain nothing.

4 Love is patient and kind; love does not envy or boast; it is not arrogant 5 or rude. It does not insist on its own way; it is not irritable or resentful; 6 it does not rejoice at wrongdoing, but rejoices with the truth. 7 Love bears all things, believes all things, hopes all things, endures all things.

8 Love never ends. As for prophecies, they will pass away; as for tongues, they will cease; as for knowledge, it will pass away. 9 For we know in part and we prophesy in part, 10 but when the perfect comes, the partial will pass away. 11 When I was a child, I spoke like a child, I thought like a child, I reasoned like a child. When I became a man, I gave up childish ways. 12 For now we see in a mirror dimly, but then face to face. Now I know in part; then I shall know fully, even as I have been fully known.

13 So now faith, hope, and love abide, these three; but the greatest of these is love.

1 Corinthians 13:1–13 (English Standard Version)

To Elizabeth, Cassandra, and Tony,
forever we are bound together by love.

Contents

Foreword
by Cassandra Scavetta

Language can be traumatic. Telling a painful story means revisiting the scene of the tragedy and experiencing those moments all over again. For her courage in the face of this task, I'm proud of my mother. I am proud of both parents for daring to say that theirs is not a story solely about pain.

It is true: as individuals, we've changed. Our family has changed. Experience has forever altered our perspective. But it is not only because of death and our pain that we are transformed. It is also because of love. We've all been led here by the most powerful love imaginable.

Preface

I am a bereaved parent, and yet that label does not define me. There is no definition of who we are—for how can we define the undefinable? We are born from greatness. We are born unlimited. There is nothing we cannot accomplish when we are talking about our own consciousness. Although I believe our circumstances are predestined before our birth into this life, I also believe that our gift of free will allows us to choose how we react to these circumstances. We cannot reverse time, but we can re-interpret what has occurred.

This book is not about grief. I don't take solace in hearing about another's suffering. However, I do take comfort in learning how others have made positive choices in their lives and how those choices have led to *real* change. I have met many people who have experienced loss—especially parents—who feel they honour their loved ones by suffering. There is a time to grieve, but no one dies so that others can suffer for the rest of their lives. I choose to honour my daughter, and honour how she reached through the veil to help me, by feeling joy and by being happy again.

My story is about the journey my husband and I undertook to open our spiritual gifts to see, hear, and feel, and to know beyond any doubt that our daughter never left our side. My story is a celebration of all the amazing and wonderful experiences that have occurred since our daughter's transition.

It is not a coincidence that you have found this book. I stopped believing in coincidences long ago. I do believe that events happen for a reason. There is a bigger picture, a divine plan. Knowing that this plan exists, we can finally learn to relax, go with the flow, and accept what happens in our lives. We can look for the hidden treasure in any circumstance. We can trust that love in any situation will be what we take with us. We can be the experiential participant and the intimate witness to the power of love.

Acknowledgments

Walking, I am listening to a deeper way.
Suddenly all my ancestors are behind me.
Be still, they say.
Watch and listen.
You are the result of the love of thousands.

—Linda Hogan

I am grateful for all of the people who have been in my life. When I think about who contributed to the writing of this memoir, I think of all the people I have come in contact with up to this point. Everyone has made an impression on me in some way.

Thank you to those who have come to my School of Miracles and have sat in my classes or received a reading. I have learned from each of you. You helped me heal. Without you, I would have no one to share my passion with. By teaching, I became the student. Each time I shared a story or taught a lesson, I was reinforcing for myself the truth that Spirit works in our lives. I have become stronger.

Thank you to all who have sat in my circles. Getting to know each of you has been a privilege. I loved the process of witnessing each of your divine sparks come to life over the weeks. I loved to see each individual's uniqueness being expressed. For those of you who were in my first circles, I feel a deep sense of gratitude, as many of you could see I was still learning, still healing. Your patience and compassion are admirable. You are all healers.

Thank you to Isabella Scavetta, who supported and encouraged me throughout the editing process. Thank you for sharing your expertise in editing the book. I am grateful that our friendship has blossomed. We are more than family.

Thank you to old friends who stood by me. It is wonderful to still have people in my life who knew Elizabeth.

Thank you to Judy Petursson, who got me out of the house in those early months. Thank you for sticking with me, even though I was no fun to be around. Thank you for helping me find Áki, my Icelandic horse. He is the love of my life, a true blessing. He helped me heal and continues to do so.

Thank you to my nursing friends in paediatrics at Trillium Health Centre, who continued to support me even though I was no longer working at the hospital. I remember the first time I laughed after the accident; it was because of you. It meant so much that you reached out to me during those hard times. Thank you to Mary-Anne, who sat with Cassandra in the hospital while we attended Elizabeth's funeral. Knowing you were there allowed me to focus on Elizabeth.

Thank you to Tom, who called me every day for months after the accident to check on me. Your friendship helped tremendously. Thank you for making us all laugh. I am forever grateful.

Thank you to Michael Reist, who taught Elizabeth English at Robert F. Hall C.S.S. Thank you for your support for more than a decade in choosing the yearly recipient of Elizabeth's Memorial Scholarship for English. And thank you for your support in promoting Elizabeth's short-story contest to your students each year.

Thank you to Kelley Potter and staff at the Caledon Library for renaming the short-story contest in Elizabeth's name. Thank you for being a part of her continuing presence in our community. I look forward to the annual Elizabeth Scavetta Memorial Teen Short-Story Contest awards night where I get to read her story.

Thank you to my spiritual teachers, especially Miriam Toste. Your patience, knowledge, and laughter helped Tony and me in more ways than I can explain.

Thank you to my family and my close friends, who listened patiently as I shared my angst of writing this book. I am blessed to have you in my life. I bet you thought this day would never come!

Thank you to Jesus, who is my rock. His unwavering love for me gave me hope when all seemed lost. Thank you to my spirit guides, helpers, and angels who continue to encourage and support me. Thank you to The Council, who continue to show their faith in my abilities by working with me. Thank you for all the messages and guidance sent to me and through others to keep me on the path.

Thank you to my husband, Tony, whose endless patience and love give me something solid to lean on. Our love can endure all things.

Thank you to my daughter Cassandra. You gave me something to live for when I couldn't live for myself. I am honoured to be your mother. I am awed by your strength and ability to love. I am amazed at all that can be contained in such a little package.

Thank you to my daughter Elizabeth. None of this would have been possible without you. You showed me what love can do. You showed me death is a lie. You are a great inspiration to many. I loved you before you were born and will continue to love you forever.

A Door Closes

When one door closes, another opens; but we often look so long and so regretfully upon the closed door that we do not see the one which has opened for us.

—Alexander Graham Bell

I'm sitting in the front seat of the cruiser. It's dark and cold. I have my cell phone in my hand. I'm trying to remember my friend's number. She's at a New Year's party in the east end of the city. She could meet me at the hospital if only I could dial her phone number, but I keep pressing the wrong buttons and have to start again. *Why can't I get my fingers to work? Why can't the cop go faster? Doesn't he realize we're racing against time?*

I've had this nightmare for years now. It's always an emergency, and each time I try to dial a phone number for help, I get it wrong and have to start again, never getting the number right. My thoughts are jumbled. My mind darts from one thought to another. I'm not the one dying, yet bits and pieces of my life are flashing before my eyes. There is a panic somewhere deep inside me. On the outside, I look normal, but underneath, I am on the verge of becoming completely unravelled. I feel alone and at the mercy of those around me. My body continues to function on its own, but any higher decision making is impossible.

New Year's Eve. I had gone to bed as usual. I had fallen asleep as usual. And then an hour later, I woke up to the sound of the phone ringing. A voice on the telephone was telling me the girls had been in a car accident. My twin daughters, Elizabeth and Cassandra.

They hadn't come home? I raced through the house. The lights still on. Beds empty. I looked at the clock: after one o'clock. *They should have been home by now.*

My husband, Tony, is with me as I speed off to where the girls would be driving from. The car strains to keep up. Tony tells me to slow down. A few minutes later, we are met by a police car blocking the road. I run out of the car. A policewoman walks toward me.

I yell, "My girls are in there!"

"You can't go any farther," she says.

How calm she sounds. I argue with her, but she won't let us pass; she won't give us any information. We turn around and head for the hospital, some 10 minutes away.

The hospital emergency room is empty.

Where is everybody?

It's New Year's Eve. My pessimistic side tells me that all the good doctors will be on holiday.

"You can't go in there," a nurse shouts at me, blocking my way as I try to go into the trauma area.

"I'm a nurse," I say, but she won't let me in. Everything is confusing. Everything is difficult. I'm the woman from the farm, running around in black rubber boots—dishevelled, distraught. I'm the crazy mother you see in the movies, the irrational one who everyone has to calm down.

The clock is ticking. The panic within me is escalating. I want to know how my girls are. No answers. A nurse keeps talking about an "unidentified female."

I keep correcting her: "She's my daughter Cassandra."
Elizabeth is behind the nurses' station in the ER somewhere.
Why can't they tell me what is going on? I've lost track of time.
It feels as if I've been here forever. Finally, I'm told that Cassandra
has been flown out to the trauma hospital; Elizabeth is still here.
They are trying to stabilize her. There is time for me to see her.

I'm escorted in to see my daughter Elizabeth. She's on a
stretcher. Blood hung, tubes everywhere. She's unconscious. Her
face is swollen, but from pressure coming from the inside. I know
it's not good. I lean toward her, and I tell her, "It's going to be
okay; you are going to be all right." I kiss her on the cheek. I want
to stay with her longer, but I know she has to go—the ambulance
is waiting.

I have to be strong.

"Can I go with her?" I ask as they take her to the waiting air
ambulance.

Another request from the crazy mom.

Frozen to the spot, I'm seeing my daughter being wheeled
away from me. I'm hearing the nurse reciting rules and regulations
about people riding in the helicopter. I can't follow her words;
my frustration is building. I am deaf to this monologue. I am
searching for the word, "yes". All I hear is, "no".

Moments later, I'm alone in stunned disbelief. I am feeling my
insides start to shake. My legs are barely holding me up.

Elizabeth was sent to a hospital at the south end of downtown,
and Cassandra was airlifted to the north end of the city. I can't
believe my twin girls have been split up. It is an impossible
situation. How can I choose one daughter over another? Ever
since they were babies, I have tried so hard to make everything
even between them. If I kissed one, I would kiss the other. If I
picked one up, the other one got picked up too. I would never
favour one over the other.

So, Tony went to Elizabeth at the hospital at the south end of the city, and the police escorted me to Cassandra at the hospital in the north. I sat in the vehicle, unable to think. It was as if I had been slapped in the face and punched in the stomach for no reason—and then handed a math exam to complete. Nothing could compute.

Somehow, I got to the hospital. Cassandra was in a coma with a severe head injury, a 3 on the Glasgow coma scale of 10, but she was breathing on her own. I knew that Elizabeth had a severe head injury and multiple internal injuries. I waited outside the intensive care unit. My friend Vanessa was there along with a stranger who volunteered with trauma victims. The volunteer kept asking me what she could do for me. She meant well. I mumbled polite responses but found her annoying. I didn't have the energy to converse with her.

She has no clue what I need.

My cell phone rang. Tony explained that Elizabeth was on her way for a CT scan of the head.

Good, she's getting the care she needs.

Ten minutes later, my phone rang again. Tony spoke slowly into the phone, "Elizabeth had a cardiac arrest on the way to the CT scan. She died. I'm coming to get you."

My brain moved in slow motion, struggling to compute the incomprehensible. I closed my phone, turned to the ladies present, and informed them that Elizabeth had died. Even though my world stood still, the world did not stop. I kept breathing. Someone guided me to the hospital entrance to meet Tony's taxi. Alone, I would never have found my way. Tony and I sat in the backseat. I kept looking at the driver, expecting some chit-chat. He said nothing. We travelled to Elizabeth in silence.

We found her alone, laid on a stretcher, breathing tube and intravenous lines still intact. Lips blue, one fingernail without polish. She had a small cut on her upper left cheek, but other than that, she looked perfect. I bent down and whispered in her ear that I loved her and always would. No tears came, just a stunned silence. I watched Tony do the same.

How long do we stay here? And what about Cassandra?

We decided to head back up to Cassandra, as we didn't know if she would die too. So, we turned and walked out, carrying a bag of Elizabeth's cut-up and bloodstained clothes. My feet moved, but my mind was numb.

Cassandra remained in the ICU for a few days and eventually opened her eyes. She looked at us, cold, detached. I told her what had happened, but she had no reaction to what I was saying. We found out later that she lacked many emotions. I tried to see this as part of her head injury, but it hurt tremendously as I just wanted to reach out to her, to share our loss of Elizabeth.

I spent the next several days walking back and forth from the waiting room to Cassandra's bedside. Nurses and friends helped me to sit, take phone calls and drink some tea. Our friends filled the waiting room, creating a cocoon of support for us. They didn't ask us for anything or expect conversation. They took turns, taking up all the chairs in the waiting room. They never left our side, even though I had little to give. Without them, I would have sat and never moved. Tony was there too, but he was making funeral arrangements.

Some of my estranged family came forward when they heard the news. I was not in a position to question why they came. I had no extra energy to attempt to fix what was broken between us. I was struggling just to breathe. But I felt that they didn't have the right to be a part of this experience. They didn't know Elizabeth or love her. Only those who loved her when she was alive should have the privilege to take part in her death. You had to know who she was before. You had to know her *essence*. You had to know what was missing. You had to know how we were together, before you could imagine how it felt to be without her. Of course, they came for Cassandra too, but they didn't know her either. They couldn't compare how she was now with how she had been before. Cassandra was making steady gains, improving each day, so the staff advised us to get some sleep. The hospital provided rooms for parents to sleep in, but they were at the far end of the hospital. Although I didn't like the thought of being away from Cassandra, I thought it would be a good idea to have a shower and lie down for a while. It was my first time alone since the accident. As I went through my routine, I had a strong feeling that I had been through this experience before, that I had lost someone close to me in a previous life. I felt people were watching me, that I was setting an example. I had to get it right this time. I had to do more than just survive this experience.

Tony remained in the ICU. It was early evening, and it was dark outside. I lay awake on the bed, staring into the dark. My mind was darting here and there. Unable to close my eyes, I looked into the darkness, and there, in the corner of the room, I saw a large cluster of white lights hovering in the air.

What am I looking at?

The group of white sparkling dots started a couple of feet off the ground and ended just below the ceiling. Time seemed to stop as I stared at the apparition. Just this presence and I were in the room. It didn't last long, and then I was alone again. I felt confused but not afraid. I gave up trying to sleep and returned to the waiting room.

Unable to understand the apparition, I put it in the back of my mind, but more started to happen. One morning, around five o'clock, Tony and I were in the hospital cafeteria. The funeral home's viewings for Elizabeth had already taken place. Tony was telling me how the high school principal, Mr. Galea, had talked to him. Mr. Galea said that Elizabeth had come to him the night she died and told him she was okay. Mr. Galea said that it had happened to him before, hearing from people as they transitioned to the Spirit world. Mr. Galea had shared the story of that night and of the conversation that he had had with his wife. As Tony was telling me the story, my mouth hung open. Somehow, I already knew the story. I knew what Tony was going to say as he said it.

Had I dreamt the night of the accident? Was I recalling a dream sequence? How was that possible? Was my soul aware of all that had happened the night of the accident, even though my conscious mind was unaware?

What Is That?

Sometimes the heart sees what is invisible to the eye.
—H. Jackson Brown Jr.

While Cassandra was still in the hospital, I tried to talk to her about Elizabeth's death. I gave her the newspaper clipping of Elizabeth's obituary. She stared at it with no reaction. I didn't realize at the time that she was unable to see it. Her injuries had affected her vision. I asked her if she was wondering where Elizabeth was. She looked at me, unable to speak. She took a paper and pencil and wrote, "Like right now? Like in my dreams?"

So, she was seeing Elizabeth. Elizabeth's spirit was with her. Cassandra's emotions were childlike and innocent; I knew she was telling me the truth. Elizabeth was with her.

Nine days after the accident, we left the hospital with Cassandra. The funeral had already taken place, and Elizabeth was entombed at the mausoleum. Cassandra was able to eat and drink but still had significant effects from her head injury. She wasn't speaking. She still couldn't see clearly. She needed help walking because she couldn't find her balance. Her emotions were limited to being pleasant and following directions. Tony and I found this situation very confusing as we tried to figure out how to reach her.

The next day, Michael, my brother-in-law, e-mailed us photos he had taken of our homecoming. A strange ball of white light hovered beside Cassandra as they both sat on the sofa.

What was that? I wondered. It wasn't a reflection. It was only in that one photo. I started googling *orbs* and found similar hazy, white circles in other people's pictures. I found out later that they are spirits—energy and light without physical bodies.

Wow, could it be Elizabeth? I had faith that she was now in the Spirit world, but that was all I knew. I started noticing balls or orbs of light in other pictures we had taken. Some even had faces in them. One time I saw a cat's face. Maybe it was our barn cat that had recently died. I started to see sparkles and flashes of light—not unlike the lights I'd seen in the hospital—dart around the room. When I photographed these flashes of light, an orb would appear in the picture.

Our friends donated money toward a piano for Elizabeth's high school. Elizabeth had loved singing and playing the guitar and the piano. The school held a memorial service to officially acknowledge the piano donation. Later, looking at the pictures taken of us at the service, I could see an orb over my left shoulder. I magnified it on the computer. It looked like Elizabeth looking at me! Now I knew that she wasn't just at home; she was where we were.

When I started to notice orbs in our photos, I started to look at photos taken before the accident. There was one photo in particular of Elizabeth riding her horse in the arena: she was surrounded by orbs. Now, they are so obvious, but why hadn't I noticed them before? There is one in front of her that is the size of half the height of the arena. She was surrounded by angels, preparing her for what was to come.

There were other signs of Elizabeth's presence. In our home, her bedroom is above ours. I started to hear bangs and other noises coming from her room. I would be in the house, and I would have a strong, full-body shiver, as if a spirit was walking through me. Our dog, Melanie, would run and bark down the hallway, as if she was seeing someone, although no one was there. In the car, whenever one of Elizabeth's favourite songs would play, a bright flash of light would fill the interior. And then, the phone calls started. No caller ID showed up. The phone would ring at 1:08 a.m., the time of the accident. A partial ring, just enough to get my attention. I knew it was Elizabeth, and I would say in my mind, *I hear you! I know you are here!*

One morning, I was alone in the family room looking through Elizabeth's music books for lyrics and inspiration for the dedication plaque for the piano. I was feeling sad; nothing was catching my attention. I was immersed in reading when outside my head, loud and clear, came a voice that filled the entire room, "Hi, Mommy!" It startled me. I looked around the room. The voice seemed to come from higher up in the family room's cathedral ceiling.

I walked upstairs and opened Cassandra's bedroom door. She was fast asleep. It was Elizabeth then; it had even sounded like her.

As I sit in that same spot, writing this now, that memory is just as real and vivid as it was that morning. How miraculous! How I am blessed. Whatever she had had to do to reach through to me, she had done it. I was able to feel her presence and hear her voice. Again, she let me know that she was still here.

Precognition

*You can't connect the dots looking forward;
you can only connect them looking backward.*

—Steve Jobs

P eople ask me if there were signs or if I had premonitions
before the car accident. Looking back on our life together,
I recall moments where time stood still and I thought about the
girls and me. One moment remains forever etched in my memory.
During her last year, Elizabeth came home from school one fall
afternoon, stood outside the garage, and looked at me through
the kitchen window. We smiled at one another.

And then there were the times when I was driving the girls
home from dance class, both of them in the back seat, chatting
away and laughing. During those moments, I would think, *All is
right in the world when we are together.*

Moving to the farm, I remember sitting with the girls at the
kitchen table, looking out at the scenery. We were feeling lucky to
be able to live with our horses, and I said, "All this means nothing
if I don't have you."

There was an inner knowing of how precious our relationship
was. But there were moments of fearful insight as well. Two
months before the accident, Elizabeth was driving along a

country road that started to bend. I was in the passenger seat, and Cassandra was in the back. It was winter, and there were snow banks on each side of the road. Elizabeth caught a tire on the snow, and we started to swerve into the oncoming truck's lane. I quickly grabbed the steering wheel and prevented us from hitting the truck. We pulled over to the shoulder, and I got out. A lady in front of us had pulled over too to see if we were all right. As I stood on the shoulder, reassuring her, from the corner of my eye I saw Elizabeth's door open. She was in a hurry to get out of the car. As she stood frazzled on the shoulder of the road, an oncoming transport truck sped by and missed her by centimetres. I froze on the spot, realizing there was nothing I could do to save her.

Looking back, that moment may have been an exit point for her to go, a predetermined opportunity to leave this life. Obviously, her soul chose not to leave then. It waited an extra two months. In that time, she completed many of her writings, which I cherish, as well as other important business I am sure. She wrote a short story for the local library teen-writing contest. I remember the moment she found out that she had won. She had picked up her prize money on her way home from school. When she showed me the cheque, we jumped up and down in the kitchen. We were laughing, so happy. The contest has since been renamed in her honour. Each year, Tony and I give prize money to the winners, and I read Elizabeth's story at the award ceremony.

Every year, the girls would ask me what I wanted for Christmas, and I always asked to have some of their poems and stories. That Christmas, days before her transition, the girls gave me a little booklet of their writings, including the short stories they had written for the contest. I was touched, and knew I would treasure them always. Both had written short stories. Both stories were about death.

"What's all this about death?" I had asked.

They said, "Don't worry about it; the stories are not about you." Such happy girls writing about death: it seemed out of character.

Four months after the accident, we flew to Miami, Florida. John Edward, a spiritual medium, was there. We hoped to be among the few chosen to receive a reading. Waiting for John to take the stage, I took pictures of the room, looking for orbs. Of course, there were many there. Looking at the pictures on my camera, I could see clearly the white outline of angel wings transposed against the ceiling above us.

We didn't receive a reading, but we were able to spend time together as a family. I took the opportunity to ask Cassandra about the story she had written. Where had she gotten the idea for it? She said that she didn't know. I thought this was strange as usually writers can recall what inspired them to write their stories. The girls took great enjoyment at making up characters for their stories. Cassandra always wrote in the first person—and still does—but in this story, she presented her characters in the third person. No names, no character outlines, just a very generic story not at all like her usual writing style.

In the story, a girl who lives on a farm loses her best friend in a car accident, and the friend is buried far away. The girl then becomes friends with a boy. We stared at each other, realizing that this story was very close to what happened to Cassandra. She had lost her twin sister and best friend in a car accident. Elizabeth had been buried about one hour from our home. Cassandra had met a boy just before the accident, and he was in her life as a friend now. In the story, the girl designates a bush on the farm as the place where she goes to think about her lost friend. We had made a memorial garden for Elizabeth on the property. So, Cassandra had written a story similar to the truth *before* it had happened.

In Elizabeth's story, she wrote about the relationship between a mother and daughter before and after the mother dies. She describes how close their relationship was and how, after the mother's death, the mother visited the daughter from the Spirit world. It still speaks to me today. I learn something new every time I read it. I feel she wrote that story to help me with my grief of losing her. Her final stanza, "There can always be a happy ending," encourages me to keep going, to look for the silver lining.

Two months before the accident, I had stood looking out the window at the expanse of green hills covered with trees that were starting to turn colour. In a moment of personal reflection, I was thinking that I had so much to offer the world, being a caring person and a registered nurse. I felt it was time I branched out, since my girls were 17. However, I was reluctant to leave my comfort zone, to venture into the unknown.

Something has to shake me up, I thought.

I'm not saying my thoughts caused the accident; I'm just saying there was a knowing there.

Ask, and It Shall Be Given to You

So I say to you, ask and it will be given to you; search, and you will find; knock, and the door will be opened for you.

—Jesus Christ

Two months in (February 25, 2004), I wrote in my journal, "I had a really bad night of crying. I just don't see the point of living with this pain when I'm going to die anyway."

It was probably the worst night since Elizabeth had died. The reality of Elizabeth's death was starting to sink in. No one could help me. No one could bring Elizabeth back to me. I took her cream-coloured winter jacket to bed with me. It smelled of her, and I needed something to hold. I was angry. My own childhood had been difficult. I had done my share of crying as a child. I had put that behind me; I had a wonderful family of my own. But now, I felt cheated from the love of my elder twin daughter. Elizabeth, Cassandra, and I had been inseparable. I felt sorry for myself. Love was eluding me once again. I couldn't understand what I had done to cause this change to happen. All the pain of my past was stacked into a huge pile, and now Elizabeth was on the top. The proverbial straw had broken the camel's back.

I looked out into the dark room and knew that there had to be somebody there, but I couldn't see anyone. I had run out of places to look for answers as to why this had happened. If the answers weren't in this world, perhaps they lay beyond what I could understand. I took a leap of faith.

I surrendered.

I spoke to the dark room, "I need help. I can't do this on my own. Please send someone to help me."

I cried myself to sleep around 1:30 a.m.

When I awoke at 4:10 a.m., I found the sleeve of Elizabeth's coat draped across my chest and tucked under my right arm.

How cute! I thought. *That is exactly the sort of thing Elizabeth would do.* Elizabeth would often come into my bedroom when I was reading before bed, and she would tuck me in. She always tucked the covers under my chin, as she knew I didn't like the covers close to my face. We always laughed. The joke never got old.

I woke Tony for him to see the coat, and we both agreed that Elizabeth was with us. I asked him to wake Cassandra and bring her down to see the coat.

Arriving in the bedroom, Cassandra immediately said, "It's so cute!"

The dark night of the soul had passed. I had tried to navigate through the darkness on my own. I didn't want to ask for help, but my suffering had escalated to the point where I could no longer handle it on my own. By accepting and admitting to my own limitations, I finally created the opening that Spirit needed to "get in."

A Door Opens

Where there is great love, there are always miracles.

—Willa Cather

The evening Elizabeth died, the girls and I had been watching TV. Since it was New Year's Eve, Sylvia Brown was sharing her 2004 predictions. Tony scoffed at the idea and said it was all crap. Elizabeth and he enjoyed heated debates on any subject, and this was no exception. Elizabeth stated her arguments supporting psychic abilities. Tony refused to accept their validity. I watched their discussion. Eventually Tony gave up his argument, and they ended their debate with an agreement to disagree. Ironically, it would be Tony who insisted that we make an appointment to see a medium. So we went.

Although this particular medium's waiting list is always long, her heart goes out to bereaved parents, so she squeezed us in. Like us, she had lost her daughter in a car accident. Now, as a spiritual medium, she has developed the ability to perceive impressions of deceased loved ones.

The three of us sat in a small basement room decorated with angels. She explained the process to us. We were both nervous and excited. I had no doubt that Elizabeth would come through to speak with us that day as our love bond had always been so strong.

The medium turned on her tape recorder and closed her eyes. She started giving us information about my grandmother. Everything made sense. Then she perceived Elizabeth and told us that a young girl was now connecting. She gave us a lot of information about what we had been doing lately. At one point, Elizabeth was talking through the medium to her twin sister, Cassandra, who was laughing and carrying on her own part of the conversation. The information was about the girls' shared love of the Red Hot Chili Peppers and the star tattoo that Cassandra's boyfriend had drawn on her wrist that lunchtime.

Here are my girls, laughing and talking back and forth just like they always have. A smile came across my face. I felt a glimmer of hope. Maybe we could learn to laugh again. A bridge of communication opened from the world of energy and light to our world. *What a miracle!*

Tony asked how we could continue to connect with Elizabeth; the medium suggested that we meditate. We left high as kites, but at the same time, very sad: Elizabeth truly was in the world of Spirit. Intellectually, I knew she had died, but it was still a process of truly knowing it deep down inside. Not too long after the reading, I crossed the threshold of denial. I started having dreams, and in those dreams, I knew Elizabeth had died. Sleep was no longer an escape from reality.

We ordered guided meditation tapes from John Edward, who we were familiar with from his television show. We listened to them every day. Within a month, Tony was seeing pictures in shades of black, white, and grey behind his eyelids during meditation. Clearly, being a sceptic did not prevent his development of psychic and mediumistic abilities. He wanted to understand what he was seeing, so he would share his pictures with me. For some reason, I knew what Spirit was trying to tell him, so I became his interpreter until his confidence in his own abilities grew.

The Wall Comes Down

The miracle comes quietly into the mind that stops an instant and is still.

—*A Course in Miracles*

It took me another couple of months before I could consistently sit and listen to the tapes. At first, the minute I sat still and thought of Elizabeth, I would start to cry, so I avoided meditation. However, after seeing Tony's success, I became determined to keep trying to connect with her. It took further months of practise to allow my body to fully relax. I was still in the "fight or flight" mode. Living without Elizabeth was being interpreted by my mind as an attack on my survival. I wanted to run away from this reality. Although no physical assault was taking place, my mind was telling my body to run. I struggled with persistent heart palpitations, headaches, sore stomachs, and extreme fatigue. Even taking a deep breath was a challenge. I learnt, firsthand, that the mind-body connection is real. To be able to sit and listen to meditation tapes took sheer willpower.

By June, I was sitting regularly listening to the tapes. At first I was uncomfortable and fidgety. Many times I wanted to scratch or move. Many times I questioned whether I was indeed meditating, and if I was, what was I supposed to be feeling? In spite of a myriad of thoughts, I noticed there were times when I was only thinking about the voice on the tape and what I was being asked to visualize.

As I stared ahead with my eyes closed, I started to see waves of colour flow back and forth. Mostly the colours were muted and pink. Sparkles of lights came in, and then dark shadows of those lights appeared in the same spot before they vanished. I could have let those colours mesmerize me, but I was usually fighting back the tears. The feeling of trying to connect to Elizabeth was sobering and brought the reality back each time I sat. *Elizabeth had died; otherwise, I wouldn't be doing this.* The immenseness of the journey that lay before me was daunting, but when I saw Tony's success, I was inspired to continue to put in the time to sit every day.

Finally, I received my first picture.

I was staring ahead, looking at my closed eyelids, when, out of the swirling colours, appeared a wall made of bricks. I could see each brick stacked one on top the other. Suddenly, the brick wall started collapsing; the bricks were falling. I knew it was my 'wall,' the barrier I had unknowingly created between me and Spirit. My wall was tumbling down.

Since both Tony and I were now seeing pictures, and I was seeing colours as well, we searched for a spiritual teacher. We were led to a lady who had been working with spiritual energy for many years. Our first meditation circle was so different from anything we had ever done. I had expected Tony to resist singing and holding hands with the other circle members, and if not resist, at least flinch, but he surprised me. He was all in. My awareness shifted, and I became the observer. I was laying down this moment to memory. I was witnessing someone I love expanding. I was seeing a side of my husband I had not seen before. In that moment, he challenged my own preconceived notion of what it is to be male.

I was amazed and proud to be his wife. My thoughts returned to what was happening in the circle. People were sharing what they were seeing from Spirit. Many of the circle members were already using their psychic abilities, so we felt a little left out, but we knew we had to start somewhere! If this experience could bring us closer to Elizabeth, we were going to do it. So we embraced this lifeline.

I went to see our teacher privately. I remember a session where she said Elizabeth was on my left side and my spirit guide was on my right. She placed my hands in their energy fields and asked if I felt anything. I didn't. Even though I didn't know what she meant by "feeling" energy, I wasn't at all discouraged. I knew that practise and time would help me to feel energy. I don't know when I started to feel energy, but eventually I did. Feeling energy came with sensations like chills, tingling, pins and needles, buzzing, pressure, pain, involuntary movement of the eyelids and body, feeling like someone was holding my hand or touching my face, feeling movement of my hair, and itchy ears or eyes—as well as my face and body heating up.

I continued going to these energy classes, even though I felt I really wasn't learning how to interpret what Spirit was giving me. One night, Tony attended the circle without me. A new person named Miriam had joined the circle. She told Tony that she saw a girl sitting next to him with the initial E and asked whether that made sense to him. Of course, it was Elizabeth. She told us she was starting her own development circle, so we started seeing her.

Miriam taught us the basics of Spirit communication, which became the foundation of my understanding of what symbols and colours mean. She introduced many ideas to us, one of which included a personal dictionary: a reference guide of symbols, colours, pictures, smells, and sensations between Spirit and me that I have experienced, interpreted, and understood. My dictionary is always expanding as there is no limit to what Spirit can show me. Once I know what Spirit is trying to tell me and I understand the message, I enter the information into my dictionary journal. In the future, Spirit may show me the same thing. Then, I can use my dictionary as a reference and not have to learn it again. Moreover, as I learn basic symbols and their meanings, Spirit can show me information that is more complex.

When I realized that Spirit could hear my thoughts, I started to practise talking to Elizabeth with my mind. Since the accident, I was having a hard time doing daily chores, especially making dinner. Elizabeth had loved dinnertime and would often come into the kitchen and set the table and ask how she could help. She had also loved us sitting over dinner and sharing the day together. It was a ritual we all had looked forward to.

One day, a fellow student in one of the classes conveyed the following message to me: "Elizabeth wants you to cook again." I wasn't too happy to get this message. I didn't want to go to the grocery store. I didn't want to face shopping for three instead of four. I didn't want to see the other families there. For six months, I had been avoiding this challenge.

But I did go to the grocery store, and I did buy some food to make for dinner. I was in the kitchen when I thought about how they could hear my thoughts. So, in my head, I asked, *Are you happy now? I'm making dinner.*

Suddenly, the under-counter lights slowly started to dim, then brighten, then dim, and then brighten—three times in all. I was surprised and excited. She really could hear what I was thinking!

I started practising more with working with thought. In the morning, I would lie in bed and talk to Elizabeth. I would ask her to give me a memory that I hadn't thought of in a while. I would lie still, my eyes closed, clearing my mind, and then I would start to think of something. I would stay with the thought, and indeed, a memory would come. Other times I found myself waking up with a thought or a word already in my mind. Sometimes I would have a song playing in my head. I focused on the lyrics that were playing over and over. Often, there was a hidden message. One morning, I heard the lyrics, "When the moon hits your eye, like a big pizza pie, that's amore!" At the time, the words didn't make sense to me, but when I later shared them with Cassandra, she told me that her boyfriend sang that song to her. Elizabeth was able to give me information that she knew I would share with her sister. Elizabeth wants her sister to know that she is around her and knows what is happening.

I had heard accounts of others smelling scents from their loved ones; however, I had not "smelt" Elizabeth. So, one night when I went to bed, I spoke to her in my mind and asked her if I could experience a smell from her. Later, in the middle of that night, I woke up to find the room filled with the aroma of vanilla. Three times I breathed in the scent of vanilla. It was the strongest smell I have ever experienced, complete with a unique quality that was all encompassing. I prodded Tony awake and asked him if he could smell it. He could not. It was my spiritual sense of smell that had been activated—not my physical one. As a result, Tony could not smell it. It was *my* experience. It was Elizabeth and me working together to make this happen. Before her passing, I had given Elizabeth a perfume for Christmas, which had a strong note of vanilla. Naturally, it was that scent that she had chosen to share with me.

Cinematic Connection

He who can no longer pause to wonder and stand rapt in awe, is as good as dead; his eyes are closed.

—Albert Einstein

Since that night when I asked for help, my life has never been the same. I recognized more and more that Spirit and Elizabeth were helping me. By the beginning of June, I finally started sitting regularly in meditation. Twenty days later, my morning crying bouts were replaced by visions as I awoke every morning. I could feel pressure and tingling around the middle of my forehead and started to see forms take shape as images came into view. I could see them with my eyes opened or closed, as I was not seeing with my physical eyes. I call them "my movies" as they are like motion pictures that last about 30 seconds. Some are in shades of grey; others in full colour. The colours and images are beautiful, with a quality which I can only describe as otherworldly. Some early movies were in cartoon form and were images that I instantly recognized as they captured a moment from the day before.

In my first movie, golden clouds started to form in the periphery of my vision. I saw a dove flying down, followed by rapid pictures of Egyptian hieroglyphs and symbols, along with tepees, castles, swords, and a grave with the letter *M* above it. The dove continued to fly and then soared upward, giving me an elated feeling. I didn't understand what I was seeing for the most part, but all appeared in a background of gold. I felt I was being downloaded with information. It was coming so fast that I was in a state of awe. I realized there was so much more to life than I had thought.

In another movie, I was flying with a flock of black birds. Everything was in vibrant colour as I flew into the valley ahead. To the right were black birds, and to the left were more of the same. We were flying so fast! We flew deep into the valley. I was flying so low I could see the grass and could almost touch the ground. Each blade of grass was in magnified detail, and the colour of green was a fresh bright green. The movement was a message that I was quickly progressing on my journey. The green grass told me I was growing and learning with others. Now, as I recall it, the grass was very short, a symbol for the start of my journey. The group of black birds was a symbol that I was traveling with others, here and in spirit, and that we were all the same, part of one big flock. The bird is a symbol for freedom. This journey will offer me freedom, a freedom which I will gain by understanding that there is a reality that is not of the physical world. How amazing!

The next day, a vision of large green leaves started to form and grow to fill my entire visual field. A black cat moved and looked at me from the centre. It was our long-haired black cat who had passed before Elizabeth did. They were together now. The next day, I saw the green leaves again along with grass growing; in the centre a very large male lion appeared, staring at me. The green leaves represented growth while the movement of the leaves indicated progression on my path. The lion was a symbol of strength and courage. The lion was followed first by a heart, and then by a flower with the name *Chi* in the centre (my nickname), and finally by a red flower. Flowers are a symbol of growth and can also mean an offering of love. In time, other movies followed: a turtle swimming in the ocean, the light from above streaming through the water, two brontosaurus dinosaurs walking into the dawn. These were messages of Tony and me being ancient and a breakthrough occurring. Again, the movement represented progression.

Soon I received one of my favourite movies. We had built a memorial garden for Elizabeth on the farm. Trees (fairy trees) surround a horseshoe-shaped garden, and a pea-gravel path leads to a meditation bench in the centre. Since Elizabeth was a dancer, and since we have always liked fairies, I have a plaque in the garden that says, "Quiet, fairy ballet in progress."

One afternoon, I was on our deck overlooking the garden and decided to send a mental message out to Elizabeth. I knew she could hear my thoughts, so I visualised a large heart-shaped balloon in my hand. I let it go, sailing off the deck into the sky above, and thought, *For you, Elizabeth; I love you.* I enjoyed sending her this message and hoped that she had heard me and received the balloon.

The next morning, I received a movie of the garden. The coloured visions were a mixture of pictures captured from real life to drawn imagery. Pictures of different things in the garden moved across my visual field and seemed to be taking me on a tour of the garden. Gold finches were at the feeder. Pink, glowing flowers with tutus that looked like fairies danced in unison in front of me; they were adorable and happy, an acknowledgement of the plaque. Up in the left-hand corner were tiny red hearts bleeding which is where the bleeding-heart flowers were. I was then taken to real pictures of pink lilies that were in bloom. Filled with amazement and joy, I watched the scenery playing out before me.

My eye was drawn to the bottom left corner, and I saw a tiny door open. I waited to see what would happen next. A red, heart-shaped balloon came through the door and popped up into my view and floated up. This was the balloon I had sent Elizabeth the day before. She was returning it to me. How amazing is that? As I write this, I can feel her touch my right cheek, and I have tears welling up in my eyes. These visions are timeless; they are not bound by earthly parameters. They hold all the emotion and power of love as I recall them, even years later. What love can do is truly miraculous!

For three years, I had movies every day. Many of these movies had animals in them, especially our horses. At times, I was worried that the movies would stop. What would I do without this connection? Around the third year mark, they did start to occur less frequently. And as for losing the connection: I no longer needed that daily confirmation that Spirit was around me and guiding me. As my own abilities broadened, I found validation from other sources.

I still get the occasional movie, and each one continues to be a thrill. I treasure all that are offered to me. Moreover, as I am better able to interpret the movies I receive, I have come to understand that my movies are filled with symbols and messages that are deeper than I first realized. Most messages from Spirit are layered with meaning. Now, as I look back in my journal, I can see the love and encouragement that I was given. I am still in awe and overcome with emotion. I know that each movie is a gift, and I am humbled and grateful that someone in Spirit loves me enough to take the time to send these to me. I know that some are from Elizabeth. She is showing me that she is still a part of our lives. She is not missing out. She knows what is happening on the farm and in our lives.

Pieces Fall into Place

There are no extra pieces in the universe. Everyone is here because he or she has a place to fill, and every piece must fit itself into the big jigsaw puzzle.

—Deepak Chopra

In the beginning, Tony and I didn't know where our psychic abilities were leading us. Were we supposed to work together? We decided to experiment and meditate together and listen to a guided tape. At the end of the meditation, we shared with one another any information we received from Spirit. At that time, I only understood pictures, and so I was waiting in the meditation for my "picture" to come. No picture came. Tony did get a picture of a woman crying and could see tears coming from her right eye. He had no idea who the woman was, but I was shocked! I had *felt* the tears coming from my right eye on my cheek; yet there were no tears there. Wow, we both got the same information, but in different ways. Tony saw and I felt. It was a revelation for me; as I had been trying to see everything, I was ignoring any sensations I was having. It hadn't occurred to me that Spirit would communicate with me in this way.

I continued to meditate on my own and in the meditation group. I started to notice any sensations I was having, but still didn't understand what they were trying to tell me. Naturally, it was frustrating. Why didn't they just give it to me in pictures? Tony was only getting pictures and couldn't understand most of them, so I was interpreting them for him. *Just give me the pictures,* I thought. *I understand them!* At that point, the process wasn't making a lot of sense to me.

Individually, we sat listening to the guided tapes almost every day. Most of what we were asked to do on the tapes, such as seeing spirit guides and loved ones, simply did not happen for me. Furthermore, I found that the tapes moved too quickly; I needed at least 20 minutes to relax first. But over time, I noticed that the colours I was seeing started to become brighter and more varied. Images started to form out of the colours. For whatever reason, I began to see mostly dog and cat faces. But then, birds began to fly across my visual field. Sometimes there were three birds, symbolizing the three of us progressing. The birds were telling us that we were free. Many times, I saw a horse running from the centre of my visual field to the left.

Tony and I shared our meditations and dreams. Each morning, Cassandra would ask me about my latest movie. Sharing helped us interpret what we saw as well as share in the enjoyment. The images and movies I saw were Elizabeth and Spirit communicating with me. They were guiding, supporting, loving and encouraging. But they were also instructing; I was learning how Spirit communicates. Elizabeth was teaching me. I knew that part of opening up more to Spirit, would require me to revamp how I saw life. Moreover, it would require all of me, not just meditation. I wasn't sure what that would entail, but I knew I had to become aware of the opportunities that were coming to me via other people, situations, classes and workshops. In addition, I had to keep an open mind and face my own limiting beliefs about myself. I had a strong sense that, in previous lives,

I had given up after loss. Once again, in this life, I felt the pull to give up along the way. However, knowing my past, my soul had prepared this opportunity for me and had arranged it so that I had few distractions. This time, my path was very narrow and few choices were available to me: I had to continue what I was doing or give up.

Over time, I slowly came to accept that Elizabeth would never be as she was in her physical form again. I would never hug her, kiss her forehead, brush her hair, or worry about her physical safety. There would be no graduations for her, no wedding, no grandchildren, but there would be beautiful new ways of seeing Elizabeth.

July 1, 2004. Every year we have an annual Canada Day barbecue. I didn't want to have a party this year, but I knew that Elizabeth would like it. The girls always baked when we had company. Cassandra was excited to make her maple-leaf cookies. I wanted for her to continue to have family traditions. That morning, Tony was up early taking out the patio furniture and cleaning the barbecue grill, but since it was only 5:30 a.m., I was still asleep.

I was dreaming. And then the dream changed, and Elizabeth was standing before me. She was inches away from my face. I could see every detail of her face clearly. White light radiated behind and around her. Her eyes were so beautiful. She was love. There were no words spoken, only love. I stared at her face, taking in every detail. I finally looked away from her eyes and looked at her hair. It was short and curly brown. *You've cut your hair.* I reached up and touched a curl and pushed it back and smiled. It was over. I opened my eyes. I was in my bed. The room was dark and I was alone. But I was so excited. I ran outside to find Tony: She had come! She was here!

I have had other visits like that one. I will never forget those visits because they were real, with an energy of their own. Whereas dreams fade, those visits are forever etched in my mind, and when I recall each moment, I feel the emotions once again. I have seen Elizabeth at the end of a dream, vivid and real. And I have seen her in meditation. Sometimes, she was on her horse, galloping toward me or riding across my visual field. Often, I have seen her face. Her beautiful, big brown eyes looking at me, her flowing light brown hair around her. She always makes me cry.

The New Road

When all's said and done, all roads lead to the same end.
So it's not so much which road you take, as how you take it.

—Charles de Lint

I was coming to understand that the process of opening up completely to Spirit included facing and overcoming my fears. I could no longer ignore areas of my life that needed addressing. I knew that the relationships with myself and with others were of the utmost importance. My happy family had been replaced with a family struggling with intense pain. I was witnessing first-hand how everyone processes grief differently. Tony was going through his own grief by keeping busy. He continued to go down to the barn and feed the horses and take care of our farm. In addition, he went to work every day. But for me everything had changed. I no longer knew who I was. I had left my nursing job when we moved to the farm the year before. I no longer cared about anything except looking after Cassandra. Since Cassandra had returned to high school to complete her final year, I could drive her to and from school, but that was about it. I had lost my daughter and the life that was linked with my girls. I had lost my daily routine. I had lost my vision of the future. I found myself sleeping a lot and hiding in the house.

Cassandra responded to her loss by focusing on her boyfriend and her schoolwork. Most of her friends shied away from her; they did not know how to interact with her. Her severe brain injury had affected her vision; consequently, when she returned to school, she had to be escorted to class. But Cassandra recovered quickly: her sight returned to normal, and she began to excel in her studies to the point that she was helping her boyfriend complete *his* homework. The girls were always internally driven to succeed, so I wasn't surprised by this development, but now Cassandra was accomplishing for both herself and her sister. She had immense pressure placed on her by us and by herself to be everything for everybody—the perfect daughter, granddaughter, niece, and friend. It was up to her to make up for the loss of Elizabeth. An impossible task and yet she willingly took it on. She rarely showed her grief; instead, she remained strong for all of us. I had read that children who have lost a sibling often delay their own grief to remain as a support for the parents. I could see what was happening and tried to tell her that she was enough, but she was comparing herself to Elizabeth who was now immortalized. Elizabeth would never fail again. How could she live up to that?

My mother-in-law, who loved Elizabeth dearly, cried continuously. I tried to comfort her, but how could I comfort her when I was barely keeping afloat? How was I supposed to balance the needs of others with the miracles that were unfolding inside and around me? Cassandra needed supportive parents and a stable home life. Although I didn't know it at the time, it was part of my growth to take up the mantle of healer.

Part of the healing process was my marriage. Tony and I had been together for 20 years, and because of our deep love for one another, I knew we'd be okay. It is a myth that most bereaved parents end up apart. If you were happy before, you will probably stay together. If you had problems before, your problems just got exacerbated, which might lead to separation. In my own marriage, I felt a responsibility to try to receive the love he was offering.

Tony is very affectionate and likes the closeness we share. During those early months, I couldn't bear to have him touch me or be really close to me. I could feel the pain coming from him, and his pain combined with mine grew exponentially when we were close. He was understanding and gave me my space, but I knew that at some point I'd have to make an effort.

I was lying in bed one morning with Tony. The blinds were down and the room dimmed. He moved over to me and I moved onto my side as we spooned. He put his hand on my hip. I could feel myself tighten up, but I let him. I didn't want him to be that close, but I knew I had to try or it would be more difficult to bridge the gap in the future. We lay there and I tried to relax. Our eyes were closed as we lay together. I started to meditate and could see the familiar colours swirl before my eyes. Suddenly, I heard a beautiful sound, the ringing of chimes to the right of me. I have never heard that sound before. I asked Tony if he had heard the chimes as well, but he had not. I knew it was Spirit telling me that they were happy we had come together again. I had taken an important step. I had made the choice to move forward.

Unfortunately, moving forward with my new life meant leaving behind some old friends. When I started to witness the paranormal occurrences, some friends became uneasy with me. One of my friends wanted to "get me some help" as she thought I was going crazy. It was difficult for some to comprehend that I was talking to dead people; they had no personal experiences of their own with which they could relate. One of my friends, who is a born-again Christian, was uncomfortable with me seeing spirit orbs. Although losing some friends was painful, I was learning that being spiritual involves accepting others as they are and moving on with my own life choices.

Tony and I had attended bereavement groups and psychotherapy sessions. But these hadn't worked for us. I left my therapist a few weeks into my treatment. I had shown him pictures of orbs in our house and told him Elizabeth was still alive. He either couldn't see the orbs or didn't want to acknowledge them. Either way, I knew it was time for me to move on, to make choices that worked for me.

During the first year, I didn't watch television. I couldn't handle seeing girls Elizabeth's age being happy and living out their lives—so I read. I read every spiritual book available. This time served as an opportunity to learn and build a foundation of knowledge. I absorbed some of the principles that made sense to me and some I wasn't ready to understand. I found there is a truth that is being played out in a variety of ways. I learned there are many ways to open up to Spirit. My way is only one of them.

Improving our connection to Elizabeth was more than important to us; it was vital. We gave it our heart and soul. Going to meditation and development circles became our therapy. In those circles, we were accepted for who we were, and we were free to talk about spiritual experiences. Participants further along in their development than we were received messages from Elizabeth and shared them with us. Our meditation and development circles were valid support systems. They reminded us that Elizabeth was around us, and at the same time, they helped us to improve our own connections. We continue to benefit from these circles as it is an ongoing process to improve our connections with Spirit and Elizabeth.

First-Year Reflections

*Yesterday's the past, tomorrow's the future, but today is a gift.
That's why it's called the present.*

—Bil Keane

T ony wanted to know why the accident had happened. He visited the crash site. He retrieved the personal items that were in the crushed car. He played out different scenarios. He hypothesized with the police details. No one knew for certain what had happened or why. Cassandra couldn't and still can't remember the accident. Her last memory is saying goodbye to her friends before getting in the car. Her next memory is coming home from the hospital 9 days later. We have had accounts from some mediums. The girls weren't doing anything wrong. Seat belts were on. No cell phones. No playing with the radio. No drinking. Tony's questions remained unanswered—until one night when Tony had a vision.

He found himself outside my blue Honda, the vehicle the girls were driving that night. He could hear the girls in the front seat talking about their night. They were happy, laughing. He knew what was about to happen and started screaming at them, but they couldn't hear him. Then the impact and he was back. While all this was taking place, he knew it wasn't astral travel because it felt more like a memory being played out. He was there that night, in some part of his consciousness. He was allowed to see that, indeed, they didn't do anything to cause the accident, but also that he couldn't prevent it.

Although I didn't focus on the details of the accident, I was dealing with my own memories of that night. To this day, when I am asked how Elizabeth died, I am placed in a difficult position. The first thing people say is, "I'm sorry." But then they ask, "How did it happen?" And that question invariably leads to "Who was driving?" People want to know all the intimate details even though I barely know them myself. Not once does anyone think that I might find it difficult to discuss this traumatic event of my life.

I prefer not to discuss this event for many reasons: It hurts. It puts me at my most vulnerable. It is my sacred territory. It is a time reserved for those who loved Elizabeth or loved us. It is a time reserved for those who understand what it means to have one's life changed in a moment.

People mean well. But unless they have experienced the loss of a precious loved one, they cannot understand what they are asking me to do when they expect me to travel back to the most painful time in my life. One cannot imagine what this experience means unless one has lived through it. Before I lost my own daughter, a good friend of mine lost her baby daughter. I had no idea what to say to her, so I said nothing. If I could go back, knowing what I know now, perhaps I'd know what to say and do. I know now that when we lose someone we love, we want to talk about that loved one, to tell people how amazing and beautiful he or she was and how we will forever miss what could have been.

One medium told us that a third car sideswiped the girls first, making them swerve, which in turn made the oncoming car hit them. The occupants of the oncoming car were hurt, but they never laid charges against the girls. Did they know something we didn't? Did they know that a third car had left the scene? Had the driver of the third car been drinking? It doesn't matter to me now, because I still believe that Elizabeth was meant to go. Her soul chose that opportunity to transition. Her journey here was complete. Her purpose had been served.

The morning of that first anniversary, December 31, Tony and I were lying in bed. When we are close together, our energies combine and we connect easily. The colours swirled before my eyes. One picture appeared after another. A police officer was looking at me, concerned. Tony and his mom were talking in the background, like a conversation on the phone; helicopter blades were turning. Then clouds and white light. A beautiful pale blue card with gold letters appeared; the letters were *ELS*, Elizabeth's initials. Elizabeth was showing me the night she left, telling me it was a gift. I was embraced by comfort, love, and happiness.

We went to see Rosemary Altea, a famous medium in Vermont. She gave us an incredible reading. She described Elizabeth, her beautiful smile, and the pain in her head from the accident. And then she described Elizabeth's transition. She heard Elizabeth saying, "Mommy, there they were, but I could hear you crying in the background." Her silver cord severed, she travelled up to meet her loved ones on the other side. She was happy, but she was still connected to me, and she knew I was crying. At that time, I didn't know about the silver cord: the energetic bond between your physical body and your soul that is severed at the time of death. That reading still gives me comfort, knowing that there were others to meet Elizabeth. At first, all I could think of was that no one was there, because we were all still here—that she would be alone. So not true!

The Fork in the Road

Be miserable. Or motivate yourself. Whatever has to be done, it's always your choice.

—Wayne Dyer

From the beginning, I have felt that I am experiencing many journeys at once. Not only am I developing my psychic abilities, but I am also moving through my own grief journey. Ultimately, this experience will culminate in my own growth and in a better understanding of myself, and it will broaden my soul. I know it will continue throughout the years. To date, I have faced many pivotal points that required a leap of faith on my part.

Elizabeth's bedroom remained unchanged for the first year. There was no pressure to address this, but at the end of that year, I finally washed the sheets on her bed and put some of her things in a box, because her grandmother was going to sleep in her room. At first, most of the changes I made were forced upon me. But I did notice that I was making choices that reflected my inner growth, symbols of my healing. I came to understand that Elizabeth was not her things—that she was with me now, actually more than she was before. I wanted to take physical action to reflect what I had internally come to understand.

At the end of the two-year mark, I was in Elizabeth's bedroom feeling sad; everything was still in its place. Now, I had to start living by what I had come to understand: she was alive and here; her soul had chosen to go; she was living her own journey.

I decided to be happier.

It was a choice for me to make. It was easy to stay miserable. I had a built-in excuse to check out of life. Didn't everyone know my daughter had died? It was easy to slide into the hole, as I called it, when I started feeling sorry for myself. However, I refused to believe that Elizabeth's death had been for nothing. All that I had received from Spirit could not be for nothing. Elizabeth didn't go so that I would suffer for the rest of my life. I had to honour her. I started to act like someone who had been given a huge gift. I truly felt it was a gift. How blessed I was to be given this opportunity to grow. Now, I knew, without doubt, that there was no death. Moreover, I began to find answers to other questions: How did I fit into the big picture? What was my role in this life? What did my soul long for? It is said that losing a child is the worst loss anyone can experience. Having known the worst grief, would I also come to know the best joy? I knew this potential for joy would continue to unfold, but it would require many other leaps of faith in my development.

Being part of development circles, I received many messages from Elizabeth through other people. Someone noted that Elizabeth's clothes were still in her room while there were girls who could benefit from having them. Five years had passed, and her clothes were still hanging in her closet and folded in her drawers. Her twin sister had already taken the ones that she liked. I knew it was time, but I just didn't want to dump them at any Goodwill store. If I was going to part with Elizabeth's clothes, I wanted to give them to someone who would appreciate the gift. I was ready to take this step forward, but the missing piece of the puzzle was yet to be revealed.

The next day, an article in the *Toronto Star* caught my attention. A charity called New Circles helped individuals who were in need of clothes and small household items. In particular, the charity helped young girls with prom dresses. Although Elizabeth died before her high school prom, she had attended a friend's prom the year before. She wore a dress with layers of tulle in many different pastel colours. Now, looking back, I know this was not a random event. It was her opportunity to get dressed up and go to a prom. Ironically, I remember drilling the boy on his driving skills and decided I would pick her up from the venue in case there was any drinking that night. Even then I was worried about the drive home. As I pulled open her drawers, I found her things organized and in place, just as she had left them. It was so like her. I decided to keep the prom dress; I couldn't part with it. But I did give away most of Elizabeth's clothes.

I dropped off many bags of clothes to New Circles in Toronto, and they were very gracious and respectful of how hard this was for me. I knew that by letting go of the old, I was opening myself to new possibilities. My attitude changed from being angry at having to change anything of hers, to treasuring items that had significant meaning to me, such as her writing and her ballet shoes and tutu. I realized then that the more I focused and held on to the past, the more it made me sad. For me, it was best to be in the present, where she lives and we are together.

Feline Love

The moments of happiness we enjoy take us by surprise.
It is not that we seize them, but that they seize us.

—Ashley Montagu

E xpanding my meditation practise included trying new things. I tried to meditate at different times of the day, for different lengths of time, using assorted guided tapes and music, and even silence. I meditated on the couch, outside, in the car, and in our meditation room. I focused on my third eye, on my breathing, or on keeping my eyes open, but I found that relaxing was most important. Any tension I was holding in my body was blocking the energies blending with me.

In addition, I had to set aside my own ideas of meditation and allow it to be what it is. In other words, I had to surrender to the process and stop trying to control it. Sometimes, I would ask questions before I began my meditation and sometimes I wouldn't. But every time I sat, I felt I was participating in something holy and sacred. It was a time during which I could be my authentic self. I didn't need to impress anyone as I was sitting with beings who loved me, who knew the real me, along with all of my secrets and fears. Through meditation, I grew to know more about myself. Spirit would present me with images and thoughts that would encourage and surprise me. They would present concepts to help me stretch what I understood as reality and to open me up to new ideas.

One afternoon, I was sitting in my meditation room practising an exercise to help me get to know my spirit guide. I took the time to fully relax. When I started to see Elizabeth's colours, I knew she was there. I asked her to step away for a moment so that I could ask my main spirit guide to come forward. I could sense the change in energy and colours. Elizabeth's vivid colours started to change to soft blues and the feeling became less intense and lighter. I played with this for a while. I asked Elizabeth to come close again and then to move away in exchange for the spirit guide.

I let that exercise go and stayed with Elizabeth. Soon I was so relaxed I found my head was hanging down and my body slumped. Loud and clear inside my head I heard: *I was the cat!* I was so deep in meditation that I didn't immediately open my eyes; instead, I remained in the meditation, processing what had just happened. I was shocked. I thought, *OMG, Elizabeth can blend with the cat?* I never knew that was possible.

The day before, I had been watching TV when Venus, the female kitty, came and sat on my lap. Since I was always a dog person, I had limited experience with cats, but I was learning about cats with these two orange tabbies, a brother and sister, that were living with us. I had brought them in from the barn as kittens to keep Cassandra company. At that time, we already had three dogs and a bunny in the house, but Elizabeth and Cassandra always wanted to have a cat. Sometimes, Venus would let me cradle her in my arms, but usually this only lasted a few seconds. However, on this particular evening, she lay in my arms and we stayed like that for about 15 minutes. As I told her how beautiful she was, she purred and looked me in the eyes. I called this our love fest. At the time, I thought that it was unusual for her to be so relaxed with me for so long. It has never happened like that since.

Now I know, for that brief time, Elizabeth had blended her energy with the cat, and we were able to spend time together in each other's arms, exchanging love. Had I known that at the time, I probably would have ended up crying and ruining the experience.

I still think about it and am amazed that it was possible. And what other times has something similar happened without my knowing?

Cupid, the male kitty, is special in his own right. He would come up to me when I lay on my bed for a nap. He'd come as close as he could and lay his full body on my stomach, his paw over my heart. I had a special song I would sing to my little boy. He helped me heal.

One afternoon, Cupid was lying beside me on the bed. I was stroking him for a while and then closed my eyes. I began meditating. Soon pink energy swirled in front of my eyes. A feeling of love and comfort came over me. Suddenly, in the midst of feeling content, I saw the canopy of one of our tallest trees. I was looking at a motion picture in vivid colour unfold before me. The tree's leaves were green and the sky blue. A flock of white and gold birds appeared above the tree and landed gently on its branches. It was beautiful, calm, and serene. I had tapped into Cupid's consciousness. In that moment, we were one, and I saw what he was thinking about.

Canine Angels

A dog will teach you unconditional love.
If you can have that in your life, things won't be too bad.

—Robert Wagner

Since I was little, I have always had dogs. At the time of Elizabeth's passing, we had three Shetland sheepdogs, one of which was named Scarlett. Within that first year, I noticed that Scarlett's health was declining. I don't know whether my own energy affected her. I know family members are affected by each other's energy, and I have seen pets mirror the health of their owners. It was difficult for me to face another death, to have another part of Elizabeth's life here change. Although I knew that Scarlett would be okay, that Elizabeth would be there for her, I didn't want her to leave me.

When Scarlett could no longer eat on her own, I fed her by hand. For a month, I mixed her food with water and filled a syringe that I would place in her mouth. I know now that I was just prolonging her death, but at the time, I felt she wasn't ready to go; her tail still wagged when she saw me. When my neighbour's sheltie died, I was given a movie of a dog lying down; two angels descended from heaven and picked up the dog. They ascended, dog in hand. I knew that my neighbour's dog was okay, that the angels had come to take her. I took comfort in recalling this vision as I witnessed my own dog's decline and impending death.

My last day with Scarlett was special. I had wrapped her in a blanket as it was a chilly spring day. She had not been down to the barn in such a long time; it was a favourite place for her. Carrying her, we walked down the path toward the barn. She immediately perked up, interested in where we were going. We sat in the tack room together, saying goodbye to the cats, the familiar smell of the barn in the air; after one more time around the stalls and arena, we went back up to the house. I was ready now to let her go.

After Scarlett's death, I received a movie from Spirit. The scene opened in front of me, bright white light in the background. Scarlett stood, tall and proud, by a riverbank. A large boulder was beside her. She turned to look at me. I had the syringe in my hand. She turned away, telling me she no longer needed it. I knew she was okay.

A couple of years later, our second sheltie, Tara, became ill. She died at the University of Guelph after two operations. Although the operations were successful, she couldn't breathe without assistance and eventually went into respiratory failure. She was the dog that loved everybody, and everybody loved her. She was pure love. Soon after her transition, she started to appear in our meditations. We would see her waddle into view, with her tail wagging.

A couple of days after Tara's passing, Melanie, our last Sheltie was coming into the bedroom to sleep; I had turned to look at her coming through the door when I saw a bright ball of gold light bounce and move in front of her. I knew it was Tara. Tara was always first into the bedroom at night. Later, Tara came to me in an even more pronounced way. She came in a visitation.

I was dreaming one early morning when all of a sudden I was in the barn. Everything was bright; the energy was immediate and important. Tara was inches from me. I was looking at her and somehow I was on the same level as she was, so we were looking straight at each other. Her black eyes sparkled and her tri-coloured coat shined. She was young and healthy. She had never looked so good. I could see in my peripheral vision that the barn's aisle was filled with people. People I didn't know; people who had come to see Tara. Wow, I realized that other people loved her too and that she knew so many people, perhaps from different lives she had lived.

But for now, she was here for me. We looked into each other's eyes, and I felt the love I have for her. I spontaneously started to play an old familiar game we used to play together, just the two of us. The next moment, we were at the door of the barn, and she was ready to leave. I wish I had asked her a thousand other questions, but only one came to me, and it came from my heart: *Tara, the next time you come back, can you bring Scarlett?* I was looking into her eyes.

They started to move to bring emphasis to the words that she spoke. Although her mouth never opened, I could hear every word loud and clear in my head. She replied, "No, it's up to the instructor."

My eyes opened, and I was back in my bedroom. I struggled to understand what had just happened. Wow, Tara came to visit, and I could hear everything she said! Instructor. What an unusual word to use. A more common word would have been master or owner. Through this new word, Tara helped me understand animals in heaven. Of course, if they had people to care for them here, they would have people to care for them in heaven. So, the instructor decides whether they can visit or not. We still see Tara every so often in our meditations, but she has never come to me in a visit like that again.

Two Souls, One Heart

Sisters, different flowers from the same garden.
—Author unknown

Having finished high school, Cassandra was now busy at university. During the week, she lived in residence, but on the weekends, I would pick her up and bring her home. She was still recovering from her head injury and had frequent headaches and bouts of fatigue. I knew university was a stressful adjustment for many students. I didn't want her to spend her weekends in an empty residence where she might feel alone. She had difficulty assimilating into the social aspect of university as she was still learning to live without her best friend. Being with Elizabeth was easy. Being with an identical twin, who was naturally attuned to herself, required little effort. When Cassandra compared other girls to her sister, they fell short.

In university, Cassandra focused on her schoolwork and had little time to pursue meditation, but during those times when she would lay quiet, her body would start to vibrate. She shied away from those experiences, not realizing that her physical body was adjusting to the higher frequencies. There were a few times when she awoke and had visions. She saw the splendour from the other side: moving images like a golden book with its pages flipping,

Sleeping Beauty from Disney—mirroring her as she lay there—and children arriving on a new shore, symbols of magnificence and a spiritual journey in progress. Like me, she also started to see flashes of coloured lights around people.

The second year after Elizabeth's transition, Cassandra tried her hand at automatic writing. Tony and I had tried automatic writing as well, holding our pens in meditation waiting for Spirit to guide them. Nothing would happen. Cassandra was determined to succeed. So, one day, she sat for two hours, telling Spirit that she would wait until something happened.

Finally, her hand started to move. At first, the pencil made large sweeps across the paper, back and forth, and then circles. It was difficult to make any sense of the writing, but over time, Cassandra has refined this ability to write words and draw pictures from Elizabeth. Before, she was not able to draw, but now she draws perfectly proportioned renditions of people, flowers, animals, and objects that relay Elizabeth's way of talking to her. Sitting in class at school, she would take her pencil and be able to connect with her sister. Both of them were writers, so it seems a perfect fit. I still find it amazing that both Tony and I are unable to do this. It remains Cassandra and Elizabeth's unique way of connecting with each other.

Although Cassandra was able to communicate directly with her sister, Tony and I continued to receive messages in meditation that were meant for her. It was the girls' birthday. I was missing Elizabeth, so I went into meditation to connect with her. I started to see her familiar colours and felt her energy draw close. A new thought came in: *Ask for a message for Cassandra*, so I asked Elizabeth for a message for her sister. I let go. Soon her colours changed, and I was seeing florescent pastel colours, shift and change, colours of blue, green, violet, pink and white. I was mesmerized. I was enjoying our time together. Suddenly, the colours changed again, and I saw words written in the air in gold capital letters:

I AM HAPPY.

Later that evening, I shared this message with Cassandra.

Surprised, she smiled and said, "This afternoon, I was sitting on my bed talking to her, and I asked, 'Are you really happy?'"

Wow! We had a good laugh. How amazing! Elizabeth had heard Cassandra's question and had made me the messenger with the answer.

The Lion

When you are going through something hard and wonder where God is, remember the teacher is always quiet during a test.

—Author unknown

There were many nights that I was suffering. Tony would ask why I was crying. I would say, "You know."

I felt I had exhausted Tony's patience, telling him how much I missed Elizabeth. We always talk as if Elizabeth is here, because she is, but I was still processing missing her in the physical. I needed someone else to talk to, so I started to pray. I had rarely prayed in the past. Now, prayer was reintroduced to us as a way to start a meditation, and in time, I became more comfortable with it.

In the beginning of this journey, I didn't know much about religion or spirituality. Although I had converted to being Catholic after the girls were born, I didn't know much about Catholicism. I understood that Jesus was our "go between," a mediator between God and us. He is someone we can give all our worries and problems to. So I started reciting the 23rd Psalm: "The Lord is my shepherd." I still don't say it perfectly, but I say the parts that mean something to me. Indeed, He has laid me down in fields of green and I have walked beside the still waters. I spoke to Him honestly from my heart and I felt better. In addition, I prayed to Mother Mary. I asked her to watch over Elizabeth as she was her mother now.

Perhaps because of prayer, beings of light started making their presence known to me. One night, when I was in bed crying, the whole room filled with pink. My body felt like it was floating above my bed. I allowed the feeling to continue and tried to stay calm. I started thinking about my guardian angel and felt she was standing behind me, cradling me in her wings. I have never had the experience again, but I know she's still with me, always loving me and always keeping me safe.

On another night, I woke and turned to see a large, male lion head staring at me. The head was huge, probably two feet high. The eyes were serious as he stared intently at me. A strong wind blew his mane back from his face, although there was no wind in the room. His mouth was moving. He was saying something to me. I felt it was a profound and important message, but I couldn't hear what he was saying. The lion faded from view, and then I saw a huge owl swoop down from above, right in front of my face. I had seen many images in my movies in meditation of gold with the letter S accompanying the lion. I felt the lion was telling me to have strength and courage. The owl to me is not only wisdom, but also a symbol of a bridge between the Spirit world and here. Perhaps together they were telling me I would be the bridge, spanning both worlds.

I called the lion my guide, and after seeing the letter *J* accompanying him, I called him Joshua. He never smiled, as his energy is about strength. He not only reminded me to have strength, but he also reminded me that I am strong. Many of my movies and meditations included pictures of the lion.

On yet another night, in my bedroom, I saw at the foot of my bed a glowing gold cross, as big as the lion. Rays of golden light shimmered out from its centre. It was beautiful and I was in awe staring at the cross as it moved closer to me. I thought, *It's Jesus. What do I say to Jesus?* I thought I would just quiet my thoughts and be in the moment. There was no time to move, as I was transfixed. The cross started moving closer to me, but as it moved, it started to become smaller. It kept moving until it reached my heart, and then I heard, "I'm in you and you're in Me." After that, the cross moved out from my heart and faded away.

Looking back, I can see how Jesus was with me all along. Of course, He is the lion. Joshua is also a sacred name for Jesus as He has many names. He does what all good teachers do: He gives me messages of encouragement when necessary, and at other times, He steps back and allows me to learn on my own. Not all of what He does is just for me, as Spirit knows only unity. So, I see what He does as an offering of learning for others too. That is why I share my experiences and all I have learned.

Almost daily, in my meditations and movies, I saw Him as the lion. As I started to cope better on my own, I started to see Him less. Now, He occasionally shows himself to me. Although He is Love, love can be tough love too. I have yet to see Him smile. I would like to see Him every day. The human part of me wants continuous validation even though I know that He is there and I don't need to see Him. Nonetheless, when He does show himself, I am overwhelmed with gratitude and joy. At the same time, I have an immense sense of responsibility; it is for me to absorb His teachings into my life; it is for me to strip away the barriers that keep me from being who I am.

One meditation proved to me that I had previously walked with Him. My eyes were closed as I lay in meditation. Suddenly, my visual field opened up, and I was looking at Jesus's feet. His feet were crossed, the right one lying on top of the left. A narrow piece of thick wood lay behind Him. He was lying on the ground, on the cross, yet to be raised. I was kneeling before Him. A strong wind swirled around me. Everything had the colour of brown and beige. The ground was dust. I looked up from His feet and saw His cloth. It was long, reaching just above His knees. It had been wrapped around Him, and the piece that came over flapped violently in the wind. The material was thick, possibly canvas, not gauze as I had expected it to be. Feeling hesitant, I stopped my gaze from going any further up.

I can't look at His face. I can't meet His gaze. The nails aren't in yet; who is doing that?

The next instant the vision was gone, and I was alone again lying in meditation. I was shocked. I was there, at the crucifixion.

What did that really mean?

Arrested Development

If you really want to do something, you will find a way. If you don't, you will find an excuse.

—Author unknown

Every spiritual journey, regardless of how it begins, almost always turns into a path of personal healing. To fully open up to Spirit, I needed to look at my personal beliefs concerning the universe and myself. If I could identify those areas that limited me, I could begin to dispel those beliefs and exchange them for new possibilities. At first, I had issues of worthiness. Who was I for Spirit to be working with me in that way? I had to unlearn my own prejudices about myself; I had to accept that I was indeed worthy of the interaction and knowledge and the role Spirit played in my life.

Although I continued to meditate and go to development classes, there came a time when I felt I wasn't improving. Too many times, I found myself sitting in class, unable to move forward from where I was. Once I sat trying to give my partner a message, but all I could see was pink. Twenty minutes passed and still nothing: no thoughts, no feelings, nothing. This became the pattern when I went to class. Although I was going to my classes and meditating at home, I wasn't learning what I needed.

My teacher saw my frustration and tried to help me as best as he could. At his suggestion, I changed my way of connecting to another's energy by placing my hands on my partner. At first, I was reluctant to change my approach, but I knew that I had no choice if I wanted to progress.

Channeling healing energy gave me time to relax and release the pressure I felt. This strategy helped, and I feel now that Spirit was guiding me in that direction. I began my hands-on healing education by learning Reiki. Later, I became certified to practise Reiki, but I remained sceptical that I would indeed use it outside my mediation circles. Then, one day, I was in the paddock with two of my horses.

We had just moved them into a different paddock. I was giving them their grain for the day. I placed the buckets down, one for each horse. Suddenly, one horse reached over and bit the other horse's muzzle. I had put the buckets too close together! His muzzle was bleeding and torn, so he quickly withdrew to the shed. I was in a panic as I ran after him. I looked at the carnage. It was my fault. But then, I quickly realized that I indeed could help. I placed my hands on his muzzle and repeated the power symbol out loud three times. I held my hands in position as long as he allowed. A minute later, he turned from me, and I left the paddock, still feeling responsible for the incident. I had caused it to happen, but I had helped in the one way that I could.

The next day, I returned to the paddock and looked at the injured horse. Nothing. I could not see any sign of blood or torn skin or any abrasion. I was shocked and ecstatic. The Reiki had worked! This event encouraged me not only to continue practising Reiki on myself, on others, and on animals but also to continue learning about Reiki so that I could become a Reiki master.

Although I had learned Reiki, I still felt I wasn't progressing in the circle. I still had periods of being stuck, especially when I wasn't performing healing. To learn more about myself, I had a Reiki treatment by my teacher. I had three pictures while I was on the table. One was of me running really fast down a lane. *Was I progressing rapidly?* The second was of me cooking in a village in the middle of a stone circle. Here, everything was the colour of dust, including my very simple covering. Suddenly, a man who I couldn't identify ran up to me and hit me on the back with a brick. Was it a glimpse into a past life of mine? The third picture was even more disturbing. I was looking at myself lying on a healing table. Up above was a spinning vortex of blood coming down into my heart. Under the table, the blood poured out onto the floor. Was my heart in need of healing? In time, I came to know the real meaning of those messages.

I have a very poor intuitive sense of people. I prefer to see the good in others. I often give people too many chances to make up for any transgressions toward me. I let go of people reluctantly. My husband, on the other hand, has a very good sense of people and can pinpoint their true natures rather quickly. In spite of his insights, I still find it difficult to believe that people don't act with the best of intentions.

Part of the spiritual path involves acknowledging what no longer serves you and moving into another experience. This involves trusting yourself and what feels right for you. I was offered many experiences to understand and learn just that. One lesson I had to learn was that just because someone gives you a message from the spiritual realm does not make that message true. Always, you must filter information through your own heart and discard that which does not resonate with you.

I had three consecutive dreams during this time period. In each dream, I was getting dressed in a wedding dress, preparing myself for the ceremony. Getting married marks a new phase in one's life. It took Spirit three times to tell me that I had to move on from my current teacher. I was reluctant to do so. I loved my time with him. When I told him that Spirit had guided me to leave his circle, he was not supportive. With hindsight, I should have considered his response with suspicion. But preferring to see the good in people, I trusted him. He had approached Tony and me for money, suggesting that we go into business together, offering spiritual classes. I saw his idea as an exciting possibility, but Tony saw this venture as a potential money pit. When Tony confronted my teacher with the truth, that it takes more to run a business than good wishes, the teacher became angry and defensive. I was very disappointed that the venture I had imagined wasn't going to work out. Later, when I found out that he had disappointed many people, I was disheartened.

When I look back at the pictures Spirit had given me, I now know their true meanings. They had told me to run fast, to leave quickly! They had shown me a man hitting me on the back, my teacher betraying and hurting me. He was bleeding my heart of its vitality and draining me. At first, I could see no harm. But the truth did reveal itself to me, and I did accept it.

Forgiveness and Gratitude

Gratitude bestows reverence, allowing us to encounter everyday epiphanies, those transcendent moments of awe that change forever how we experience life and the world.

—John Milton

In my search to understand what Spirit was giving me, and to move past the feeling of being blocked, I travelled to England to attend the Arthur Findlay College (AFC) for spiritualism in Stansted, England. Tony had attended months before and had had a great experience. I needed new experiences and teachers if I was to develop further. At AFC, there are no newspapers or television; students are immersed in an environment of learning from 9:00 a.m. to 9:00 p.m. At the beginning of our week-long stay, we, the attendees, are placed into different circles, each taught by a tutor. When not working with our tutor, we can attend various workshops.

I was placed in a circle that met daily in the Blue Room. Sandy Baker was our tutor for the week. She quickly put us at ease with her great sense of humour. When she told us that she was an expert with feelings and colour interpretation, I knew I was in the right group! In the first exercise, we were paired up and asked to scan our partner's body.

I sat with my eyes closed and visualized my body being hers. I focused on the top of my head and slowly moved my way down my face, waiting for a feeling, picture, thought, or colour. At my forehead, as I stared at the inside of my eyelids, I saw the colour change to green. I had no idea what that meant. *I'm stuck already!* I thought.

I called Sandy over to help me.

She asked, "What does green tell you? It could be that the person likes nature or that there is growth for her right now."

I looked at my partner, and she said, "I love nature." In relaying the message, the colour changed, and I was able to move to the next piece of information coming in. A buzzing and tingling was happening around my chin. *Did my partner wear a retainer?* I discounted this information as it came too easily. Next, I moved on to a picture in my mind's eye of my partner walking with sandals on rough terrain. Her toes were exposed; she was scared to move forward because she might get hurt. As I shared this information with her, everything made sense, including the retainer! I had moved past my block. Because I had understood the first message, Spirit was able to give me another message.

Later in the week, I was in the chapel where a mediumship circle was just coming to a close. I overheard a man complaining to his tutor that he wanted to not only see Spirit but also feel Spirit to know they were there. *How ungrateful*, I thought. But then I realized that's how I appeared when I complained that I was not getting pictures: ungrateful. A lesson learned.

I thought about my own abilities to feel Spirit. When Elizabeth came to me, I could feel her deep emotion, which often made me cry. Then my body would be flooded with warmth. I might feel a touch on my right cheek. Colours of pink and violet would swirl in my vision. I could feel her hugging me.

Midweek, we were sitting in meditation in the Blue Room.

Soon after we started, I saw the colours turn to bright gold. An outline of a figure stood before me. I was full of energy. All kinds of buzzing and tingling were going on. Clearly, inside my head, I heard, *Forgive yourself.*

In that moment, I was immersed in love and felt that it was Jesus talking to me.

I was shocked. I had no idea I had to forgive myself.

How could I be responsible for what had happened? But thoughts had come to my mind. *Why did I let the girls get their driver's licences? Were they fully prepared to drive so young? What if I had delayed the licences? Why didn't I know country roads could be dangerous? Was I pushing the girls to succeed?* Such thoughts served no purpose other than to torture me and to keep me in the past. I had to let them go; I had to forgive myself. I was not responsible for what had happened.

Later, I learned that there were deeper issues within myself that needed to be forgiven, old hurts and regrets that needed to be abandoned, but that learning came much later.

When the Student Is Ready, the Inner Teacher Appears

All are called but few choose to listen.
—A Course in Miracles

I n the fall of 2006, I started giving weekly classes in my home. I felt I knew enough about meditation and how to interpret spiritual messages to help others get started on their own journeys. I was inspired by my previous teachers and by some of the exercises, prayers, and organizational strategies they had used. At first, I took their best practises and incorporated them into my own circle. However, I still needed a lot of guidance from Spirit, so, although I began each session with an idea of what I would be doing, I essentially let Spirit guide me, which was 5 percent me, 95 percent Spirit. In time, the practises I had borrowed faded away and were replaced with others that felt right for me. I had found my own confidence, my own authenticity.

Earlier that year, during the summer, a few friends and I got together to practise giving messages from Spirit to one another. One friend saw a card for me that had 10 hearts and a white lily on it: this meant 10 people would be coming to my circle and death or loss would be a common element.

But how much of my own action was necessary to bring people together for my first circle? A thought came to me to put an ad in the local paper, announcing the formation of this group. I felt it was important that I participate or put action into my desires. That way, I would know that I had done my part. I didn't expect Spirit to do it all for me. I was part of the team. My participation was important. Little did I know that my own goals were coming head to head with a mighty foe.

It was a warm August afternoon. Tony and I were out on horseback, riding along a path through fields of hay. The grasses were tall on each side of the path. The wind blew the blades, making it difficult for the horses to discern whether the grass was moving due to the wind or a predator. We were trotting along when we came up to a bend in the trail. Suddenly, the horse in front of me took off at a gallop. My horse immediately bolted forward, dislodging my feet from the stirrups. I gripped with my legs as we bolted down another straightaway. My husband and his horse turned abruptly into the field of grass, hoping to slow the horse down. I, too, turned and pulled on the reins to follow. I don't remember hitting the ground.

I woke up and tried to stand up. My vision was blurry, and I was disoriented.

What's going on and where am I?

I took a few steps forward only to find pain flooding my body. I lost consciousness and collapsed on the ground. Some 20 minutes later, I awoke at home lying on the floor. Everything was blurry. My head hurt. I had a sense that I had lost time. But then I thought, *If I lost consciousness, why didn't I get to see Elizabeth?* I was disappointed! It would have been cool if I had had an out-of-body experience.

Blood was pouring from my ankle where something had pierced my boot. Tony was beside me.

"The ambulance is here," he said. In the ambulance, someone kept telling me to open my eyes. I didn't want to; what if I couldn't see?

Tony and I were left alone in a room, with me on a stretcher, waiting to see the emergency room doctor. My sight slowly started returning to normal. I started to give myself Reiki.

What does having this accident mean? I wondered. There are no accidents in life, so why had this one happened to me? Although no horse is completely bomb proof, I had a relatively safe, level-headed horse. No immediate reason came. Many scans and X-rays later proved I had a concussion. I came home to a cracked helmet, bruises, cuts, and questions. Three days later, the revelation came.

The concussion had left me tired and weak. I needed to rest to allow my head to heal. I thought of my classes starting in a few weeks and wondered whether I would be able to lead them—and then it hit me! I had done it to myself. Here was a perfect excuse *not* to start the circle: I wasn't well. I had had a concussion! I had given myself the perfect out.

My ego was getting scared. If I started my circle, my path would be well underway to helping not only myself to heal, but others too. However, healing meant uncovering the truth about myself. This is not a happy territory for the ego! If I found out who I really was, the ego would die, as the ego is about the illusions we hold about ourselves.

Well, screw that! I wasn't going to allow my insecurities and doubts to rule me. I firmly felt I was meant to teach others; furthermore, I already had experienced much joy in sharing my stories. I was not going to allow myself to get in the way of me. It all made perfect sense.

My first circle consisted of 10 people, most of whom had lost loved ones, including children. One of the ladies present explained how she had come to be with us. She rarely read the local paper, but one day she felt an impulse to pick up a copy, and she saw my ad. She showed the ad to her friend. Both had decided to attend the circle and share the loss of their children. Spirit and I had indeed worked together to make that happen. My intention was to create an atmosphere that would facilitate personal growth in the individuals, either by assisting them to communicate with their loved ones and Spirit helpers or by having them meet others in the circle who would help in some way.

I have learned over the years that those who come through my doors receive whatever it is that they need for the next step on their journey, regardless of what that personal journey may be.

Tony sat in on every class. He provided me with the support I needed. I could always count on him to bring through a message for someone or to bring humour to the situation if the energy got too serious. He was a role model for the men in the group. He too liked the opportunity to practise giving and receiving messages with Spirit. Often, he would see loved ones in Spirit, eager to get a message through. He facilitated many moments of healing.

As the months progressed, it became clear that Tony had a gift for mediumship. He frequently saw spirit people in his meditations as well as in those moments when he closed his eyes, relaxing. They followed him to the bathroom at night and looked at him as he drifted off to sleep. They must have been attracted to his light, and they must have known that he could see them. He continued practising his mediumship in class and with friends. He took every opportunity to practise. He started to sit professionally and give mediumship readings.

I wanted to expand my own mediumship, so later that year I travelled to the Arthur Findlay College for the second time. I needed new learning experiences. I wanted to expand my understanding of channeling, healing, and leading circles. I wanted to gage how much I was able to do with Spirit and how

I could improve. Although my second visit at the college wasn't as life changing as the first, it helped to confirm what I already knew to be true about myself and my path, namely, that I have a compulsion to share my experiences and to tell people that they can communicate with their loved ones. At AFC, I took every opportunity to watch the tutors with their students. I wanted to see how they led circles and workshops, so that I could gain new ideas to bring into my own circles. I went to the workshops where I could practise my mediumship skills, and I came home with new confidence.

Upon my return, I was excited to share what I had learnt and practised. After I said the guided meditation in my next circle, I sat with my eyes closed and asked Spirit if I could give a message to each person in the circle. Nothing came.

I was confused, but then I heard a voice say, "It's not about you." I was shocked at first, but after my initial disappointment at not getting my way, I smiled and thought, *Of course!* My ego was trying to take over so I could show everyone what I was able to do. That's not why I led circles. I sat back and allowed Spirit to lead the rest of the evening. The members took their turns sharing the messages they received during the meditation. The last lady looked at me and said, "I was given a message to give for each person; may I share?" I laughed inside and thought, *I love how Spirit works.*

A year later, I developed a mediumship practise circle of my own. Up until then, I had been passing on the mediumship readings to Tony since he was better at these readings than I was. It can be difficult to practise mediumship once you know your family and friends' loved ones in Spirit, because you already know so much about them. First, you have to set aside what you already know so that you can receive some new information about them. However, I realized I could not improve my mediumship without practise. So, when I saw others in my circle wanting to increase their confidence in mediumship, I realized that I had found my opportunity to improve. Every week, the circle of students and I gave messages to two strangers who would sit for us. I saw my students' mediumship skills and my own blossom. Not only were we learning, the strangers who sat each week for us were being introduced to the concept of mediumship, and in most cases received messages from their loved ones.

Hearing from Elizabeth had helped us heal, and now we were providing the venue for others to heal on their own grief journey.

Clicks and Lights

The Prince of Peace was born to reestablish the condition of love by teaching that communication remains unbroken even if the body is destroyed, provided that you see not the body as a means of communication.

—*A Course in Miracles*

I'm not sure when it started, but within a couple of years after I began teaching, I started to hear clicks in my left ear. I had already heard sounds and familiar voices calling me. Sometimes I would hear *Heather,* not knowing who was talking to me, but these "clicks" were different. Moreover, Tony and Cassandra didn't hear them. Sometimes the clicks were soft; other times they were loud. Sometimes there was only one and sometimes several in succession. At first, I thought it might be like Morse code, but after experimenting with that possibility, I realized they weren't. I often heard clicks while driving. They were my cues to pay attention. They warned me of accidents up ahead, of turns I was about to miss. A visual aid while driving would be too distracting, so a sound guided me.

More importantly, the clicks served as a confirmation for me. The clicks happened primarily when I was talking or thinking about something that was important. For example, one day I was having lunch with a friend. I was explaining how everything comes from the heart when I heard a distinct click. Sometimes, I would hear clicks when we were talking about Elizabeth or sharing memories of our family.

I often heard them when either I or one of the participants in my classes was speaking about something that was worth acknowledging. So I often said, "I got a *yes* for that!"

Although I have heard Elizabeth in meditation, speaking inside my head, she usually communicates with me through clicks. I find the clicks are really helpful when I am teaching; they remind me that Spirit is present and that I am being supported.

At this time, I rarely hear clicks in my right ear. Once, while having a past-life regression, I could hear faint clicks in my right ear. Perhaps this was a Spirit guide who chose to communicate through the other ear.

Along with hearing clicks, I started to see a pale blue light. It always appeared in the same position, near the centre of my visual field. It often moved to the left and then disappeared. I felt this small light was Elizabeth on her horse. In meditation, I had seen Elizabeth many times on her horse, so I knew it was her way of telling me she was there. One time in class, I saw her light and asked her to come closer. The light started moving toward me. It became bigger as it approached. There she was, sitting on her horse! I smiled.

When I was developing my mediumship in my circle, I realized that the flashes of light I was seeing around people while my eyes were open or closed seemed to be telling me something. Elizabeth's blue light was always in the same position in my visual field. I started to reference this field as a clock. Elizabeth was always in the nine o'clock position, but close to the centre of the circle, where the hands would begin.

During mediumship readings, I would see other people's

lights in different positions. I knew that Elizabeth was 17, so I knew that if a light was above her, that light would be an adult female, and above that, an older female, like a grandmother. The closer to the centre of the clock, the closer they were to the person. They were family, not friends nor distant relatives. On the other side of the clock, at the three o'clock position, were males. The same held true, in respect to age. Under that position were children and way down near six o'clock were babies.

If the lights showed up in the perimeter, they were people who weren't very close, like an acquaintance or stranger. Twelve o'clock would be ascended masters (people who have lived on the Earth before and have mastered a virtue or a discipline), the upper right quadrant would be animals in Spirit, and the upper left would be spirit guides and angels.

Some lights were white; some were black. Others were deep bright blue—those were people still living that Spirit wanted to say hello to. Elizabeth taught me that because her light consistently started in the same position at nine o'clock. Since movement indicated progression, the movement to the left told me that we were progressing together. Movement to the left is the future; movement to the right is the past. I often saw Elizabeth's light beside people in the class. She was working with them. She was also telling me that they were mediums. Whenever I saw her light, I told her in my mind that I knew she was there to validate her effort to connect with me.

After Palma, my mother-in-law, transitioned, I started to see a white light above Elizabeth's blue one. The two of them are together once more.

I Am Not My Body

In these instants of release from physical restrictions, you experience much of what happens in the holy instant; the lifting of the barriers of time and space, the sudden experience of peace and joy, and, above all, the lack of awareness of the body, and of the questioning whether or not all this is possible.

—A Course in Miracles

After teaching in the house for a year, we decided to build a studio above our garage. Our intention was to provide a private space where I could teach meditation and development classes and Tony could offer mediumship readings. This project would also show our commitment to what we were offering people. *If we build it, they will come.*

We released this plan to the universe, knowing that we had done our part. We named our new venture "School of Miracles." I remember sitting at the kitchen table with the builder we had chosen to work with. Elizabeth was busy getting my attention. For about 15 minutes, she kept clicking in my ear. Clearly, she was excited! I knew we were making the right choice.

Since the studio area was pre-trussed from the builder of the house, we had little choice as to the size of the studio or where the stairs would go. There was a small space next to the stairs that looked like the perfect place to put our pyramid energy system. The pyramid must be aligned to true north. As we were putting it together, we noticed how tight the space was going to be. There would be no wiggle room. The walls grazed the sides of the pyramid. I placed the compass on the pyramid, and it perfectly aligned to true north. We laughed. *It's a sign*, I thought.

With the pyramid energy system, the person meditating enters the full-size open pyramid, lies on a mat, and holds quartz vajras or hand wands in his or her hands. The pyramid provides an optimally balanced energy to meditate in.

I had a profound experience during my first time meditating in this pyramid. I had my earbuds in and was listening to meditation music very low. I was lying on the mat and holding the quartz vajras. I started to slip into deep relaxation. I could see the colours flow in front of my eyes. A feeling of letting go came over me. I felt I was floating. I could no longer feel the massage table beneath me or my hands. Waves of soothing energy were passing under my hands and body. I lost track of time. Somewhere during the meditation, I heard heavy footsteps coming up the stairs. Then, I heard the clinking of a dog collar on the wood floor as a large dog lay down. I was aware that this was happening; however, I was too deep in meditation to respond.

The next moment, I was sitting on the table with my legs over the edge. I was still in the pyramid, still in meditation. *My body is lying down, but I am sitting up.* I was the same person. Nothing had changed. I could still feel, think and see. I was still myself, but I was having this amazing experience!

I could see only what was immediately in front of me. A man came forward, standing inches away from me with his chest at eye level. I could see his nubbly white sweater. He leaned close and gave me a hug. I could feel the texture of the sweater against my cheek as he leaned in. I could feel his love toward me. I hesitated to look up into his face. I wasn't ready to see it. I also didn't want to do anything to cause the experience to end.

Is it Jesus? Is it Tony's soul?

A moment later, I was back in my body. I struggled to make sense of what had just happened.

One morning, shortly after this experience, as I lay half-awake in bed, I heard a German shepherd dog barking. I don't know why I knew it was a German shepherd, as we had never had this breed of dog before. With our shelties passing away, there was an opening for new dogs in our lives. Tony had always wanted to have a German shepherd. He had been trying to convince me to get a new dog, but I wasn't being receptive to the idea. I didn't want to start over with a puppy and sacrifice the time that it would take from me.

Tony had been telling me about a puppy he was looking at and showed me pictures of it online. He had already been talking to the breeder. I wasn't happy about this, and he eventually dropped the idea. But I knew, hearing this dog bark, that I had to get the puppy for him.

I went to the computer, found the breeder's telephone number and rang her right away. She said she would hold the puppy for Tony. Later, that day, she e-mailed me back and described her horror at arriving at her father's place where the puppies were being kept and seeing Samantha, our puppy, leaving with another family. She quickly intervened, setting the people straight and offered them another puppy. If I had not taken Spirit's guidance, the dog that Tony had had his heart set on would not have been there.

So, perhaps the man with the dog was Tony's soul coming to congratulate me for taking this big step, for opening the studio. I have not had another experience like this one, but I do wonder, *Is that what it's like to die; to no longer be your physical body, but to continue having real personal experiences just the same?*

A Deeper Level of Trust

*I will awaken you as surely as I awakened myself, for I awoke
for you.*

—A Course in Miracles

School of Miracles allowed an array of new opportunities, not only for other people but also for Tony and me. We continued our personal development by inviting guest teachers to the school. One of my friends told me about Moira Hawkins, a medium from England, who would come over to teach at our studio. We invited Moira to come, and she came.

At the time, my mother-in-law was newly diagnosed with cancer. She was struggling to adapt to the news that her cancer had spread and that it was now in two locations, stage 2 cancer. One evening, Moira, who channels messages from her guides, brought through advice for Palma. They told her to live her life and continue doing the things that she enjoyed. Although this was only a small message, it was exactly what Palma needed to hear. She needed to know that she had permission to continue to live and that she should not assume the role of an invalid. As a result, she lived the remaining three years of her life to the fullest. I thanked Moira for her ability to bring through this important message for our family.

While at School of Miracles, Moira gave workshops on mediumship and trance/channeling. Those workshops not only helped me with my own teaching but also introduced me to trance. Trance is the ability to blend with Spirit so that they can use the physical voice of the channel (the individual in trance) to communicate with the sitter (the person sitting for the reading). It is different from mediumship as communication is only in one direction—from Spirit through the channel to the spoken word. Mediumship, on the other hand, is often a two-way communication—mediums can ask questions in their minds to the spirit person to help clarify and understand the information received for the sitter.

During the trance workshop, we practised sitting and holding the energy of a higher being of light. The goal was to hold or blend with those energies while remaining relaxed and focused. While holding such energies, the channel can experience very intense feelings, such as pressure, rapid breathing and heart rate, flushing, involuntary movements of hands and arms, and rapid eyelid movement. The sitter may notice these affects as the channel experiences them.

Because the energies are uncomfortable, many people consider them to be bad energies and so discontinue developing trance ability. Different bodily sensations are not necessarily bad sensations. Over the years, I have found that these feelings range in intensity from quite intense to mild, depending on my own energy field at that moment. I feel Spirit modifies how much energy they need to transmit depending on how I am feeling that day. If I am low in personal energy, they may have to ramp up the connection. At the beginning, when I was learning, the energy was very intense for me, maybe partly due to needing validation— if I didn't feel anything, how would I know they were there?

As I blended with trance energies, I stopped thinking and

relied more on feeling. I accepted the process of letting go of control and allowed the energies to merge with me. I started to notice that a word would fill my head. The hardest part of learning to channel can be saying the first word. At first, only one word came at a time. It took trust and experience to know that the next word given and spoken would make sense. I don't understand the mechanics of transferring information from the higher realms, where all is present at once, to our linear process. The words that I spoke sometimes came slowly and other times came more quickly; I could not control how the words came.

Although I enjoyed the challenge of learning new avenues of working with Spirit, learning to channel was a long process for me. It was a journey of many layers of trust that I had to go through. After Moira went back to England, my husband, my friend Deb, and I started our own trance circle and met once a week in the studio. We were excited by this new endeavour and didn't know what to expect. Week after week, we sat in meditation and then took turns speaking. Many times, we blended with these energies only to find that we were unable to speak any of the words given to us. We continually received messages from Spirit, informing us that we were trying too hard. Looking back, I know this was absolutely true. Part of our problem was our expectations. The other barrier was our self-doubt: we didn't believe we were good enough or capable of being channels for Spirit. Spirit is highly intelligent and knows what is good for the channel's development as well as what is best for the audience. Perhaps we weren't ready to bring through those higher concepts and needed more experience—or maybe the timing wasn't quite right.

We had been sitting in this circle for about a year, when the fall term was starting at School of Miracles. I was teaching the psychic development course, explaining to the students what the difference was between inspired speech and channeling. During my explanation, I started to feel the familiar trance energies come close to me. My voice deepened and slowed, my heart started to beat faster and my breath quickened. As the energy intensified, I started to lose my own ability to put together thoughts. Spirit was definitely getting my attention! I knew that they were present and that they wanted to speak. However, I was reluctant to proceed; I didn't feel I was ready. I wanted to hone my skills at channeling in my own little circle where it was safe to make mistakes. This was one of the many times in my development where I had to take a leap of faith. It was my choice whether I was going to progress with channeling after my many failed attempts. I had had so many wonderful experiences with Spirit leading up to this night that I had faith that they would not let me down. They were choosing to work with me now, so I trusted and asked the class if they would allow me to channel for them.

That night, my husband, who was usually in class, was not present. His absence was not accidental. Sometimes his presence made me feel self-conscious, as I wanted to do my best when he was witnessing my work. I played the meditation music low to give my mind something to focus on. I asked everyone to stay seated so as not to distract me. The room was full of anticipation. It was a significant moment for me.

I closed my eyes to help focus on the task at hand. I was breathing fast; there was so much pressure on my heart that I felt it was going to leap from my chest. I could see the colour of pale blue behind my eyelids, while a bright energy was moving toward me in the 12 o'clock position. This energy became brighter and moved closer to me. I started to recite a prayer in my head, that God would surround me with his angels of protection and that I would communicate with only those of the highest love and light. I held onto that intense energy, cleared my mind, and allowed them to take centre stage. (To help me to "take a back seat" and minimize my interference, I imagined that I was sitting to my right and slightly behind myself.) My hands started to rise up in front of me and my fingers stretched out and made involuntary movements. It took too much of me to control them, so I left them to do what they willed. The energy was so strong that I thought I was going to levitate. I summoned all of my willpower to sit still, knowing that 12 sets of eyes were on me.

I swallowed and felt the energies calm slightly. My lips parted in preparation for speech. The words came one by one and continued for about 10 minutes. None of it made sense to me. As soon as the words left me, I was unable to recall what I had said. I stopped myself at a certain point as I felt holding this energy was just too much for me. I opened my eyes and asked if anything I had said had made any sense. There were many head nods, and one person said it was exactly what she needed to hear.

This experience left its residual effects on my body. I had feelings of shivering although I wasn't cold. It took a while to return to normal as my breath slowed and my heart returned to its natural rhythm. I was exhilarated and awe struck as I felt the immensity of what had just happened. I didn't care what others thought, as I knew this was an important moment for me. The difference from being in our trance circle to being in front of the class was that I had the audience that Spirit had wanted to speak to. There were reasons for this channel: someone needed to hear what they said and I needed the experience.

When I first began channeling, I wasn't sure who I was channeling, but I had a definite benchmark of how loving energies would behave. They would never *take* me over. They would never pass judgment on anyone, including myself. They would never identify anyone by name in their channel (out of respect for another's privacy). They would be willing to speak through me when another was in need. They would bring through higher knowledge to guide and support. The group I was channeling always displayed those loving qualities. However, after a few months of channeling, I finally said that I would not continue unless they revealed their identity to me. I sat with my eyes closed in front of my circle and started to see my grandmother and Elizabeth come into my visual field. I knew it was all right. My grandmother and Elizabeth were saying it was good. I didn't get the answer I expected, but I did get the support I needed to continue.

As my channeling progressed, the information coming across became more specific. Channeling was a team effort between the energies of Spirit and myself. The information coming across was a unique compilation as they were blending with me as an individual with my own experiences, knowledge and references. In spite of my successful experience, there were times when I remained reluctant to channel, because it took energy and courage to attempt to channel in front of my students. But my students persuaded me to try, and so I did for them. It took many, many months of practise before I could relax fully during the channel, thereby allowing the information to flow easier.

As my confidence grew, I went to a deeper level of trust in my channeling and allowed my audience to ask questions. Although I set this intention before I started to channel, sometimes Spirit would allow questions and other times they stopped talking after their message was completed. I wanted to progress in my channeling so that I could help individuals as well as groups. Spirit knew of my desire. After a year of channeling for groups, I was in the studio with a lady who was waiting for Tony. Tony was late. Tony was never late. It dawned on me that perhaps Spirit had set up this opportunity for me to channel for her. It was my choice if I wanted to take this chance. I did channel for her, and the information that came through resonated with her.

Over the following months, while in channel, I received information about who I was channeling. I knew they were good, as they were highly respectful toward myself and the others who were listening. The information coming through proved helpful for the group. Moreover, Spirit remained respectful of me and never *took me over* whenever they wanted. There was always mutual consent. When I felt their energy close, I assumed they wanted to speak and so allowed time at the end of class to channel. Later, I learned that they are always there if I allow the channel to take place.

I channel *The Council*, a group of ascended masters who have walked the earth before and who have mastered a virtue or a discipline. This group works at the soul level. And since there are many who make up The Council, different beings from The Council will come forward for different individuals, taking into consideration the individual's needs and the being's expert guidance. To keep it consistent for me and to help me trust who I will be giving a voice to, the male energy that represents The Council always makes the initial connection with me.

The Council helps us plan our lives before we are born into this current life experience. This plan is sometimes referred to as our pre-birth plan. They help guide us throughout our lives and are there as we transition back into the Spirit world at the time of our physical death. At that time, we will have an opportunity to meet with The Council, as they surmise for us how we progressed on our goals and help determine what would be the next optimal experience for us in our next experience.

As I progressed into individual readings, they would often talk about who the recipients were at their core and how this core essence was being expressed in this life experience. I have never given two readings that were the same. Every time I channel I learn more about how our unique energies are being expressed here on Earth and how we are part of the fabric of life. We are not complete without each other. Each of us plays an integral part in the formation of the whole; without one individual, we are not whole.

Over time, how I receive information has expanded. Because I am able to see spiritually or am clairvoyant, I usually start the channel with a picture The Council gives me. The Council does not talk about the pictures, but uses them to help me understand the information that is coming through. Once the channel is completed, I share the pictures with the recipients to help them understand what The Council is saying. When I was learning to channel, I was told that I should not see pictures. I'm a big rebel when it comes to rules: I don't like them much! I have found that we should use our gifts in the way that is most appropriate for our level of understanding and to keep an open mind in developing further abilities. Spirit will use our gifts, in isolation or in combination, in a manner which is unique for each of us.

My channeling has evolved over the years as I reach a deeper level of trust. I still see the familiar blue energy come toward me, but the changes in my breathing and heart rate are very subtle. Now, I can channel without the confirmation that comes from the intensity of energy. Perhaps my own energy field has changed or risen so that I am nearer their vibration, thereby requiring less energy to make channeling happen. In spite of these developments, there is a limit to how many readings I can channel since channeling does take substantial energy from me. I've learnt through trial and error that I need a short break between each channel if I am giving individual readings in succession. If I don't take a break, an intense pressure in my chest develops.

Once, I took the opportunity to give short readings at a psychic fair. There wasn't time to go into full channel for each person, so I connected in and received information on where each individual was in his or her life at the moment and what steps each needed to take to progress. Although I was working with The Council's energies, I was not speaking their words. This strategy took less energy from me and allowed me to work with many individuals. My own levels of trust and willingness to try something new have proven vital in expanding my abilities to connect with Spirit.

After Easter 2013, I gave a workshop on mediumship and decided to give the students a channel to close the day. I prepared for the channel in my usual way: I said a prayer and set the CD to record. I took some deep breaths and relaxed. I started to blend with my familiar Council energies. I sat with the energy for a while and then allowed the words to be spoken.

> Welcome, we are The Council. Each of you holds the light. Indeed the light can be dimmed and it can be brightened. And so, now as we speak, your light is shining in various degrees. Some of you have a large light and this light reaches out to many others, and it has come to pass that indeed your light is being noticed by many, who not only walk with you, but those who do not know you and yet feel a remembrance when they gaze upon your face.

The energy changes, and one steps forward to speak.

> **Loved ones, do you not understand that each of you holds the key? That each of you has what another needs? Can you not reach out to one another and give from your**

heart, give what you have freely without reserve? For you cannot take the material possessions with you, for these are of the world and have their own time of existence. And so yes, they serve a purpose, but release them, for they cannot go where you are going.

There are many who are in need of love, for attention, for someone to notice them. Take their hand, look in their eyes and give them the dignity that they so deserve. Keep your head up; see life around you; it is there for you to notice. Each of you will expand the self in many different ways, and this is how it should be. And so, although you can be inspired by others, you must do what feels innately right, for the self. For you know what it is that brings you happiness and contentment and fulfilment. But I can tell you, that if you do not make a connection with one another, then you will not find yourself.

Just as in the days that followed my return, there were those who had faith, who walked forward and gave freely to those around them, who spread the good word. There was much resistance, and you will find it true today, but know too, that there is much hope in the world, and you can expand what I started. For it is in loving one another where the power lies, where the joy is, where the peace is. At any time where you find yourself hesitating to give your love, you will find yourself suffering. And so, we hope that as you learn this, you will understand that as you give love freely, you also give permission to yourself to be happy.

There are many lights that shine on the earth at this time, but there is a ways to go. Once you have worked on the self and understood how you can shine your light, then perhaps it is time that you shared with others more. If you have not found your light, then perhaps it is time that you learnt about your soul's purpose, about why you are here, about what it is you need to understand. And so, can you see how there are those who are just understanding the self, then there are those who have already worked through this and are at the position now to share, to teach, to help? This is a process different for each of you, and so honour where you are right now, for you cannot leap ahead.

Each of you has been anointed. Each of you has been given gifts and abilities. Each of you knows the truth. Trust, have faith, know that I am always with you. Know that this cannot be any different, for we are bound with one another from the beginning of time.

Hold each other's hands. Now, take one another's hands. [The circle joins hands.]

This is our brothers and sisters. Get used to feeling one another's hands in yours. This should not be alien to you. Have strength to reach out. Have strength to share what you know. Have strength to open your heart. There is no other way.

There is a book that has been written, but know that there is a fresh book, one that has yet to be written. And so, yes, there has been a past, but know that you create what is to be and what is to come. Enjoy, have faith, learn, grow, experience, touch one another, share, love.

As I was channeling, I knew it was Jesus speaking. It had been a dream of mine to channel Him. He had finally come forward for me—or had *I* finally allowed Him to come forward for me? His energy was solid and strong. Although I had been ready for this experience, I remained hesitant to channel Him again. The responsibility was immense. Could I allow myself to work so closely with Him?

Although I struggled with being worthy, I have channelled Him again. The Bible informs me that Jesus works through people who are less than perfect. So, once again, I am learning my lesson of trust. I trust that whoever comes forward from The Council, including Jesus, will be perfect for both me and the recipient. I demonstrate this trust by allowing future channels to be what they need to be. I do not try to channel Jesus. Instead, I allow the most appropriate Spirit to come through for the recipients of the message.

Palma

Every loving thought is true. Everything else is an appeal for healing and help, regardless of the form it takes.

—*A Course in Miracles*

S even years after Elizabeth transitioned, my mother-in-law, Palma, died of cancer. She never understood Elizabeth's passing although she herself was seeing visions after Elizabeth transitioned. Palma was very religious and prayed the rosary every day, a ritual she enjoyed since it gave her solace. I remember her with her Italian prayer book on her lap and her rosary beads in her hand as she recited the rosary over and over. She did not realize that she was engaging in a form of meditation and that this ritual provided a foundation for the visions to happen.

Before Elizabeth's passing, I wanted to understand Palma's devotion to her faith. I was searching for a higher meaning to my life when I converted to Catholicism after the girls were born. Often I am asked to explain the differences between religion and spirituality. People tend to think of choices in terms of black and white. My experiences have shown me that I can take a little from many religions and incorporate those teachings with my own beliefs. I know now, beyond any doubt, that there is a living force in the world and that love never dies. I understand now that Palma's recitation of the rosary provided her with a sense of security as it brought her closer to God. Even though, through her visions, Palma saw Elizabeth happy and beautiful in the Spirit world, she continued to grieve for the loss of her granddaughter and prayed to join her.

In short, Palma struggled with her religion. She couldn't reconcile her experiences with her spiritual sight and the teachings of her church. She doubted my explanations of her visions. She found it difficult to believe that Elizabeth was happy and that all was well. She could not absorb and understand the knowledge she had been given, and so it remained an internal conflict for her. As her illness progressed, she did take comfort in believing that Elizabeth would be there to greet her, so I do feel that her visions served to comfort her eventually.

Five weeks before Palma died, there were many miracles in our lives. Needing pain management, Palma moved from hospital to her daughter's house for care. We witnessed her decrease of consciousness as the morphine doses increased. I wanted to reach her, but she was slipping in and out of this earthly experience. Every time she closed her eyes, she would talk to the spirits in the room and comment on how she was seeing beautiful scenery. She was having experiences on the other side. Her hands would move as if she was busy cooking or sewing. We asked her what she was seeing, and she would exclaim, "Awe, such beauty, it's beautiful." These were not hallucinations; she was seeing the other world. When we told Palma that it was okay for her to go, she would reply, "I'm waiting for Elizabeth."

One evening I was meditating beside her when I saw a ring of people surrounding her bed. A tall man in a brown hat and coat stood at the foot of her bed. I asked them why Palma was still here.

I heard, *There are people who love her and there is a process to this.* It was true that we were hovering around her, hoping to see a glimpse of her old self come through with a look or comment that was familiar.

I leaned close to her so she could hear me. "Did your dad wear a hat?" She said for sure he did. I told her that her father was here.

I wanted to see more of Elizabeth during those weeks, but I felt Elizabeth was standing back so as not to confuse Palma into thinking it was her time to go. I wanted to do more for Palma. Many times, I wasn't even sure whether Palma knew I was there beside her. At home, every night before I went to sleep, I would ask for information about Palma. *What did I need to know about her?*

One morning I had a vision. As I awoke, I looked into the bedroom and saw in front of me, like a movie, a young woman with long dark hair, walking through the customs lines at the airport. Although I could see only the back of her and not her face, I knew it was Palma, her younger self. Going through the airport was a symbol of the process she was undergoing during the last days of her life here.

Tony wondered why he wasn't getting more information about his mom. But then one day something happened. As Tony has a rare blood type, he gives blood regularly. He was at the blood-donor clinic, and the nurse asked him to sign and date the usual consent form. He dated it August 19, 2010. The nurse was shocked: it was July 26, 2010. He didn't know why he wrote that date, but he knew it was significant.

Palma remained with her daughter, Teresa, who controlled Palma's care. Teresa embraced every treatment available to save her mother, even though prolonging Palma's life could mean prolonging her suffering. In doing everything she could for her mother, Teresa, too, was going through her own process and coping the only way she knew with her mother's impending death. In many ways, Palma's dying was more about the living and their understanding of life and death than Palma's own transitioning.

Two weeks before Palma died, I had another vision of her. She was still at the airport. She was standing on a platform at the top of the stairs of a ramp, ready to embark the plane. Being from Toronto, I was used to seeing enclosed ramps leading to the plane, but this was an airport where the passengers walk outside across the tarmac and up the stairs to the waiting plane. Palma stood on the platform at the top of the stairs; she looked around, taking in all she could see, one last time.

Later that morning, Cassandra and I went to Teresa's house. We were eager to climb the stairs to Palma's room. I told Teresa that Palma was having one last look around before she went. We found Palma sitting up in bed and smiling. She was chatting away and telling us everything she had been thinking about for the last few weeks when she had not been able to verbalize. She talked for a couple of hours. We listened and laughed at her unique mixture of Italian and English. The phone rang and she talked to her many friends. It was amazing to see her *back*.

The day came to a close, and Palma again returned to her deep sleep, where she continued to mutter about what she was seeing. She progressed into a deeper state of unawareness where she remained unable to respond to us. Once again, I was looking at a dying woman. Unfortunately, Palma's care was not in my hands. Her daughter and I disagreed as to how to keep Palma comfortable. I left that day determined not to visit Palma again under these circumstances. Seeing Palma suffering was torturous for me. I hoped Palma would understand my decision to give her daughter space. My answer came more beautifully than I could have imagined.

Two weeks elapsed. Early one morning, I was in a dream where I was just about to lead a mediation group. I stepped out of the room to look at my cell phone to see if there was any news about Palma. (My anxiety was even playing out in my dreams.)

As I was looking at my phone, I looked up and saw Palma come through double doors.

I asked, "Palma, what are you doing here?"

She was matter of fact. "Uh, I came to see you!" She knew I hadn't been to see her in the past two weeks! I watched her float in, her customary limp absent; behind her, red roses floated all around her. She was wearing a black dress with black lace across the front and down both arms. I had never seen that dress before. She sat down without assistance. I knew she had something to tell me.

"I want to make sure you get …" And then I couldn't hear what she said. I sensed her daughter was beside her, although I couldn't see her.

She said to Teresa again, "And make sure she gets … and …"

I don't know why I couldn't hear those words. I awoke knowing that she had come to me. It was 5:00 a.m.

Later that morning, Tony and I went for a ride with the horses. We ended up at the local diner in the village and had a leisurely breakfast. His phone rang. It was Teresa.

"Mommy's trying to talk; I think you should come and see her," she said. We had become accustomed to these daily calls: Teresa, in a panic, fearing that today would be *the day*. Tony said he'd go to see his mother. Somehow, I had nothing pressing to do that day, so I said I'd go with him. Although I had decided never to return to Palma as she lay dying, I felt no hesitation in going now.

When we entered the room, I knew that today would be the day. Palma's breathing was laboured. She was unresponsive; her organs were failing. We sat and watched her struggling to take each breath. An hour later, she took her last breath. As I gazed at her face I saw Elizabeth, her familiar blue light shining beside Palma's head, and then they were both gone. Elizabeth had waited for the last moment to come forward and assist her grandmother to the other side. It was August 19, 2010, the date Tony had written down three weeks earlier while donating blood.

Later that day, we visited the funeral home to go over the plans for the service and entombment. Palma had previously arranged these services, so there were few decisions to be made. The funeral director mentioned that there was no request for flowers. I immediately asked to see their book of floral arrangements. As I opened the book, on the first page was a glorious spray of red roses to be displayed on the closed half of the coffin. I instantly knew this was what Palma wanted. After the church service the next day, we took the flowers to the entombment ceremony and gave each person who visited her crypt a red rose. We had exactly enough.

Beginning with the service the next day, Tony and I have seen Palma in meditation and felt her presence often. The message she was trying to share with me in my dream came rushing back to me one day when her daughter was trying to determine which pieces of her jewellery to give me. Teresa showed me a large gold medallion necklace, but I knew it wasn't the right one.

"Make sure you give her …" I heard Palma say again in my head. I finally saw the one she wanted me to have. Years ago, I had relayed a message to Palma from Billy, a student in my class. Billy had brought Palma's mother through in Spirit. Her mother knew that Palma often wore a smaller gold medallion around her neck. Billy could see Palma rubbing it between her fingers. Palma meant for me to receive this small saint medallion and the gold cross her mother had given her.

Weeks later, Tony and I were watching a movie we had rented. The movie was about a funeral director who could see and talk to the recently dead in his care. The recently departed did not believe they were dead and would argue with him about their condition. He comforted them and let them know that indeed they were deceased. In the scene we were watching, a dress was delivered for the person to wear in her coffin. He unzipped the bag and showed the dress to the deceased lady. I gasped! It was the dress that Palma had worn in her visitation with me the day she transitioned. The movie was about how the deceased are okay and how life continues for them and their loved ones. I felt it was another message for me, another confirmation that all is well. How did Palma know that Tony and I would rent this movie? I find that intriguing and wondrous!

During the time I was not visiting Palma, I woke one morning with a song playing in my head. It was Michael Jackson's "Black and White." I was expecting more information about Palma's condition and couldn't understand the song as it would pertain to her. The next day, I heard Melanie, my last surviving Shetland sheepdog, being sick. I rushed to her side and felt the heat coming from her body; her ears seemed to be on fire. I rushed her to the vet. Melanie was unable to walk straight and was running a high fever, indications her organs were failing. I didn't want to let her go. She had been with me for 13 years, longer than any of my dogs. Affectionately, I would call her *my little old lady*. Although the vet knew it wasn't going to help Melanie, she put her on intravenous fluid for the afternoon to see if she would improve. The vet knew that it would give me time to process what was happening and the impending decision I would have to make. I returned to the vet's a few hours later with Cassandra and Tony. When they saw Melanie, staggering around the room, they looked at me. I couldn't see it. I didn't want to see the truth.

Months after Melanie and Palma had departed, I was struck by the parallel between Teresa and myself and finally understood Teresa's motivations concerning her mother's end-of-life care. I had never cared for someone close to me who was dying. The closest I had come to this experience was with my animals. I realized that I couldn't understand what Teresa was going through as her mother lay dying since I hadn't been in that situation myself. Teresa had been reluctant to let her mother go. She had difficulty seeing the truth about her mother. I had been reluctant to let Melanie go. I, too, had difficulty seeing the truth about Melanie. Spirit had tried to tell me about Melanie's condition with the song. Melanie is black and white. But I was too focused on Palma. I couldn't see that it was Melanie they were talking about. It was the perfect lesson for me in so many ways.

Discerning Energies

Painful as it may be, a significant emotional event can be the catalyst for choosing a direction that serves us more effectively. Look for the learning.

—Louisa May Alcott

When teaching classes and workshops, I am often asked about protection and lower energies. I respond with a quote I've heard often, "As above, so below." In short, there are people here that do not like you; the same holds true in the Spirit world.

There are many who have stopped their development over fear of connecting with unwanted energies. However, many factors come into play. Some people will have those encounters and some will not. Some of those interactions will be for the understanding of the soul while others will be for the understanding of the energy communicating with you. I can only speak from my own experiences.

My goal in sharing my experiences is to let people know that it is possible to communicate with Spirit. I do not teach some information and withhold the parts that can be difficult to talk about. I share everything I have learned in the process, including what I have learned about Spirit and myself.

In the early stages of my development, I was desperate to learn everything I could, to open up fully so I could communicate with my daughter. Although I was already communicating with her in meditation and through my movies, I wanted more. I had already felt her energy near me, seen her colours and the pictures she had sent to me. I had received visitations from her. But I wanted to *hear* more. I wanted to hear her talking to me, just like a regular person. In an effort to open all my spiritual centres, I started to say affirmations, statements which reinforced a thought. Before I went to sleep, I would say over and over, *I hear Spirit.* I acted as if it was already happening.

Finally, one year later, just before Christmas, I started to hear, around my left ear, people singing Christmas carols. The singing was especially strong in the car or as I was falling asleep. I thought, since Elizabeth likes to sing, that it was her. I also thought, since the singing was about Christmas, that it was supportive of Christ's consciousness. I started to affirm that I could hear Elizabeth singing and shared this development with my family.

That Christmas, we went on vacation to Paris. During the flight to Paris, I felt that the voices were getting out of control. They continued even after reaching Paris. They always spoke in sing-song and would sometimes mimic what I was thinking in my head. I would ask questions, and then hear them reply. Once, when entering the hotel room, I heard childlike voices sing, "Here we are! Here we are!" I continued to think that it was Elizabeth.

Later, during the night, when I got up to use the bathroom, I heard, "Wash your hands!" Now they were telling me what to do. There was more than one person speaking, always in song. At first, I thought it was a choir, but when words were spoken, they sounded as if they were spoken in unity with other voices. The voices became more aggressive and annoying. They knew I could hear them and that I was reacting to what they were saying.

One morning, they called me a "bad" girl. I was shocked. Up to that point, the voices seemed to be supportive of me. But now they had changed and were out of control. Later, when I had a cold, I asked them to leave me alone so I could sleep, but they didn't. I knew then they weren't good energies. They had no respect for me. Unfortunately, by listening and talking to them, I had established a relationship with them. I had been so desperate to hear Elizabeth that I had left my intuition and good sense behind. Not knowing any better, not knowing how it should be, I had accepted the voices.

On the plane home, I looked over at Cassandra sitting next to me, and saw an ugly black spiky thing hovering in front of her. It looked a lot like a Klingon vessel from Star Trek. When I closed my eyes, I could see specks of black moving in my energy. These specks had no light and no form, per se. I started using different strategies to get them to leave me alone. They were very noisy when I tried to fall asleep. They would taunt me, saying, "You aren't worthy." When I told them that I didn't want to talk to them or listen to them anymore, they became angry. Sometimes, at night, I would feel painful pokes. I got scared.

I started asking for protection from everyone good in Spirit, but nothing changed. I became confused. *Where was everyone? Why was no one helping me?* I asked people who had been communicating with Spirit longer than I had to help me, but they didn't have any answers; they didn't want to talk about my experience, and some didn't even acknowledge it. Suddenly, I had the plague! I have since learnt that very few spiritual teachers want to talk about such experiences.

Since Spirit was allowing this experience to happen and didn't seem to be intervening, I started to think that there were lessons to be learned. I concluded that no one in Spirit was overly concerned about what was happening to me because no harm could come to me. When no one from Spirit came forward to talk to me or to give me any ideas on how to remedy my situation, I realized that I had to find a solution on my own.

I went to a local lady who I knew who clears energies. I stood in the middle of her circle of energy practitioners, and they did energy work on me. They described seeing someone from Spirit who came into the circle and took the negative energies away. I didn't feel any different but returned home hopeful. Nothing really changed. I could still hear the sing-song voices. Nonetheless, this lady had shared words that made me feel empowered and better about my situation. She had told me that not everyone has such experiences, so I should consider them a good thing! I was on the path to knowing the truth; this experience would serve me in the future. In the meantime, I still had to figure out how to proceed on my own.

To help me sleep and to drown out any voices I was hearing, I started listening to a meditation CD on very low each night. It was just enough to drown out "the voices" and to allow me to get to sleep. Sometimes I would wake up from a bad dream, and I could hear them laughing. Sometimes I would get a vision all black and ugly. I knew it was them trying to trick me.

In time, I started to follow the law of attraction: you attract that which you think about. I needed to stop talking to them and about them if they were to cease to exist for me. I informed them that I would never do what they told me to do, so they should give up. Eventually, I came to learn that they do not know love. They cannot produce light. Everything from them is dark, unsymmetrical and ugly. They have no respect. They prey on fear. Fear gives them power.

When I told them that they were loved and that they could find peace, the cord was severed. The physical assaults, although minor, continued for a spell and then ceased.

Although this process took years, I continued to teach, love, and live my purpose. More importantly, it brought me closer to Jesus as I began to pray often. Prayer not only drowned out the chanting from them, it also helped me focus on the positive. I stopped praying from fear and started praying from a seat of power.

I know who I am. I am a child of God. It doesn't get any better than that. Nothing can touch me, for I am eternal. I know love. I am love. There is nothing to fear. When I pray, I pray from strength of knowing who I am, not from fear.

These interactions brought to my attention beliefs about myself that could have been hindering my progress. I did believe, at that time, that I was not worthy of doing God's work. If I could be manipulated by what those negative entities were saying to me, I still had trigger points that needed to be addressed. I started to delve more deeply into what I felt about myself. I have since learnt that I can do great things through Him and that I am loved without judgment. Now they can tell me all the bad things they want; I know none of it is true. I have taken the power back. They hold nothing over me.

Sometimes, in the quiet of the night, I might hear a faint, faint reminder of their voices. However, I cannot hear what they are saying. They have free will to travel and do what they wish. I will never talk to them again. I will leave those in Spirit and perhaps others on the earth to help them to know the light.

Working with different energies has made me a better person, teacher, and channel. When I started to channel, I was concerned about giving a voice to lower energies. How would I know who I was channeling? I had learnt how love felt, how love looked, and how it was to be loved from Elizabeth and from my experiences with The Council. My experiences with the lower energies taught me the opposite. I now knew both sides of the coin.

School of Miracles

Meditation is like going home.

—Heather Scavetta

I n the beginning, when I first started attending development
circles for my own development, I never missed a class. I
was too scared that I might miss something really important.
Since each week revealed a new piece of the puzzle to me, I was
afraid a class missed might mean a puzzle piece would not be
found. The angst I felt was real: What if I missed something
really important?

Of course, now I know that Spirit will do whatever it takes
to get the information I need through to me. I need not worry. I
need not be afraid. I am exactly where I need to be for where I am
going. Knowing this, in my own classes, I encourage participants
to relax and enjoy the process of opening up to Spirit.

Needless to say, I have progressed over the years. I started
out on this journey with little experience, but I have blossomed
into someone who is comfortable with how Spirit communicates
with me. What propelled me onto this path might be considered
a tragedy by many, however, I see it as the highest form of love.
Nonetheless, it was my choices, the choices I made along the way,
that led me to this moment of happiness and fulfilment.

I could have chosen to keep this newfound connection to Elizabeth and Spirit a secret, but I could not contain it. Within me is a deep desire to teach others how to recognize this spiritual connection and how to heal within this process. There is a deeper knowing, given to everyone, of what one's life purpose is. Living one's life purpose should bring joy. I know I am living part of my life's purpose because teaching and helping others bring me joy. When I see the spark of understanding in another, an understanding that I have awakened in some small way, I feel I've won the lottery! I have found an avenue through which I can teach and heal others while providing myself with a venue through which I can continue to grow and to heal.

The School of Miracles studio that we built over our garage carries an energy of its own. I do only Spirit work in the studio. There are no phones, no pets, no arguments, and no negative energy present in its space. Many who enter the studio observe that the studio feels calm and welcoming. After many years of meditation and working with Spirit, I feel the space carries a high degree of vibration. The pyramid and sacred geometry tools and the music I choose to play add to the feeling of balance.

Each week, I teach multiple development classes. I lead each class with a prayer, usually consisting of three elements: who I am speaking to, why I am speaking to them, and a thank you. Since there are many spirits, the prayer sets the intention of which spirit I want us to connect with and why we are sitting. Creating a starting point of authentic intent and trust sends out a vibration to connect with like-minded spirit beings. I encourage those present to say their own prayers if my prayer does not resonate with them.

I follow the prayer with a meditation. For me, meditation is like going home; home being our real reality or heaven. I believe that it is what everyone is looking for: to experience a spiritual connection and to know that we are loved and never alone. Over time, meditation assists the molecules in the body to hold more light. An individual's DNA will actually change or dormant strands will become activated. It is love that changes the DNA. I am forever changed. I am not who I was before I started meditating. For one, I have become more sensitive to energy. Now, I can see, hear, feel, and know when my daughter and Spirit are around me, without even going into a formal meditation.

Meditation instills discipline and is important to one's development since it involves learning how to be in a state of relaxed focus. Beginners should concentrate on relaxing the body first as completely as possible and on remaining still. The body needs to be as relaxed as possible as any tension will hinder the blending of Spirit's energy with the individual's energy. At first, the mind may wander and think of all kinds of things if it isn't kept busy. A guided meditation is perfect for beginners as it keeps their minds occupied while listening to the words spoken and imagining what is happening. This relaxed focus will eventually replace the myriad of thoughts that usually crowd the mind. Over time, the gaps between the thoughts will become longer, and there will be more time sitting without thinking. Meditation is also about sitting in the energy of love. Spirit is love. Feeling this reconnection to our source can bring about many emotions. It is normal to cry. I cried in meditation every time for the first two years. The love I was feeling was overwhelming.

Instead of reading a pre-scripted meditation to the group, I channel it. My ability to channel the meditations developed over time as my trust in Spirit increased. Since each meditation is specifically tailored by Spirit for the people in the circle, each meditation is unique and is never replicated. In these meditations, Spirit gives me not only the words to speak but also the supporting clairvoyant pictures necessary to bring to life the visual, guided mediation. Often, participants will comment that they see things before I actually speak of them or receive information that they need. This is possible because Spirit knows who is in the circle and what experiences they are seeking.

There are multiple opportunities for Spirit to work with each individual. The meditation guides those present to see something like a flower or to receive a gift by looking into their hands to see what's there. Each flower conveys its own message; the type and colour have meaning. Each gift received holds a special significance to the individual. The interactions with Spirit help to build a dictionary of symbols that Spirit can use in the future. These opportunities allow Spirit to give individuals information in a specific way, to show them how their spirit guides and loved ones work with their abilities. Do they see pictures? Can they see in their mind's eye? Do they receive thoughts instead? Since everyone can receive thoughts, this is the first ability Spirit usually uses. However, it takes time for individuals to discern whether the thoughts are their own or from Spirit.

It is a journey of trust.

Spirit is often subtle. In addition to time, it takes practise for individuals to learn how they receive Spirit's information. Most people have one spiritual ability that is stronger than the others, but many will use a combination of abilities at the same time.

Although most development occurs in personal meditation practise outside class, engaging in group work plays an important role in psychic and mediumship development. Being part of a group and doing similar work with others creates a unique energy that supports each individual. The group energy can be stronger than individual energy, and this strength allows everyone to connect easier. Moreover, since Spirit knows only unity, Spirit rarely gives information for one individual alone. Thus, sharing is important because some of the messages that are received and some of the experiences that occur are for more than one person.

Sharing messages and experiences allows for the expansion of what is possible. To this end, I strive to create an atmosphere that is nonjudgemental and safe so that after the meditation the circle members feel comfortable sharing their meditation experiences and the information they have received from Spirit. Witnessing another's accomplishments allows success to be possible for everyone. Because individuals work at their own levels of ability, those who are further along in their development serve as examples to others as to what is possible. What we see others achieve becomes possible for everyone and provides new ways of interpreting information, including symbols, feelings, colours and smells. Sharing also helps to dispel doubt. When others describe experiences similar to their own, they can recognize the reality of their own experiences. Thus, the process is validated.

After the meditation and sharing, I lead the students in exercises that help them practise working with Spirit so that the students can expand their psychic abilities. These exercises could involve psychometry, scrying, cards, giving messages to fellow students, healing work, body scanning, remote viewing, mediumship, channeling, and more. I trust Spirit to guide me as to which exercise is appropriate for the group at hand, given what the members need to learn or practise.

For further practise communicating with Spirit, I encourage students to ask a question before going into meditation, whether at home or in class. Learning to receive answers to specific questions can be a way to enter into a dialogue with Spirit. When receiving messages for others, students have the added benefit of being able to validate the information received. When practising this process in class, it is important for the recipients of the messages to be honest. It does not help the learners to think they are correct when they are not. If the givers convey incorrect information, they have to reflect on their interpretation of the message and/or how they received the message: Was it received with their own minds? With time and practise, individuals will learn how to receive accurate messages. Ask, wait, receive—this process will lead to clear messages. Reaching, striving, trying too hard, making assumptions, or guessing, will lead to only unclear messages. Those giving the messages should simply state what they saw/heard/felt instead of trying to build their own story around their message, a practise which is known as castle building. A straightforward message is often the best.

Not all interpretation has to come from the giver of the message. For example, if the giver receives the impression of a younger sister, the giver should not assume that the recipient is a younger sister. It is better to say, "I am hearing younger sister." The recipient then may say, "Yes, I have a younger sister." In short, it is okay for the giver of the message not to know everything about the message. Once trust in the communication process is established, it becomes easier to receive information, because there is less doubt in the process. Doubt can hinder the communication process by closing the energetic field through fear.

Elizabeth remains an important force in my classes. When I see her with students, I know that she is helping them or she is telling me that they are mediums, even if they are not yet aware of this ability. When she clicks in my ear, I know that she is telling me something is correct; she serves as confirmation and encouragement. I love when we are working together! Along with Elizabeth, both Palma and my father-in-law, Rocco, show up, especially in my mediumship classes where they help students practise receiving information from loved ones who have crossed over.

All students who are guided to come to me, whether it is for Reiki, a channelled life reading, psychic development, meditation practise, mediumship development, or a mediumship reading with Tony, have the opportunity to get what they need to progress in their own development and in their lives. I can only present the information to them; it is up to them to become aware of how Spirit works in their own lives. The following is an example of how Spirit can bring about the connection that we often seek.

One morning, I had meditated, asking Spirit to share with me what I needed to know for the day. I started to think about a pendant. I didn't know what the pendant meant until later that day when my friend Heather shared the following with me.

"When getting ready today, I got out something I sometimes bring with me when going to one of your classes. I don't think I have ever shown it to you. It reminds me of Elizabeth. When I was first learning, she was the first one to come through that really rang true and I knew it was real. Sometime after that first learning experience, I was in Goodwill. My cart was stopped when my wheels hit something on the floor. I looked down and there was this little ornament. I thought of Elizabeth right away; I may have been thinking of her—I don't remember now.

"I had it out today to put on a new chain to wear as a pendant as it is Christmassy, but I did not remember to get the new chain. I did not realize until I got home from our lunch that it was in my pocket! I wonder if this is why you were thinking of a pendant. If I am feeling down and see this, it always makes me smile and I feel better.

"I will always think of Elizabeth as my first spiritual teacher. I still remember the images she gave me. She showed me the stirrups of her horse, and you told me she was always fussing with the stirrups to get them just right. She showed me her strict ballet teacher and a makeup mirror that you have, and she gave me the impression she was with you when you were using it. When we filled and expanded our meditation balloons in class, the air was filled with pink, a favourite colour of hers. I am grateful to her."

This story is just one example of how Spirit works with my students and me every day, whether we are inside or outside the classroom. The first step in benefiting from what Spirit has to offer is to become aware that we are all connected. This connection makes everything possible. The second step is to become aware of what is happening in our lives on a moment-to-moment basis. There are no coincidences. Everything that happens is the result of syncronicity: the outcome of Spirit at work. The more we trust this process, the more we will notice how our lives are being supported by Spirit and the more we will know that we are loved for who we are.

There is an important third step as well. It is one thing to understand that Spirit and our loved ones are with us, however, it is another thing to allow this knowledge to change us. We must apply our knowledge to our lives; without application, the knowledge we have remains as thought. There needs to be a change from within that affects our thoughts and actions so that we verify that we are living this new knowledge. Without application, the change remains dormant and unlearned. In applying spiritual principles, there is actual growth and progression in the person. Spirit sums up this development perfectly as they shared this concept in a channelled message to one of my students who is a bereaved mother.

Question: "I feel I am on the edge of going forward to do something, and I am wondering if you can give me some clarity as to what that might be."

Answer: My dear one, we see your struggles of the heart and know that these energies constrain your health as well as your ability to interact with others. You can move forward by accepting where you are even though you want to be in a different space. You cannot move forward without acceptance. This may feel like a threat to you and you may for a short spell feel like you are going backward. But if you do not experience this, you will create a circle of continuance where you will continue to reach forward, retract, and then start again—because you are moving from the same energy. We understand that it is difficult. We are not minimizing your experience; instead, we wish you much love. Can you accept the love that is being offered to you, now, in this moment? For if you can, then you will see barriers fall away. Can you trade your sorrow for our love?

In this message, The Council is telling this bereaved mother that until she accepts the death of her son, she will always be operating from the same state of mind she is in currently, that of non-acceptance, regret, and lack. Accepting the situation changes not only how she will see herself, but also how she will see the world; moreover, it will lead her to make choices different from the ones she is currently making. From her present state of non-acceptance, she makes the same choices that continue to lead her in a direction that leaves her unfulfilled; thus, she ends up back in her current situation, her mental state, unchanged. Once she truly accepts her life as it is, including the death of her son, she will make future choices that will have a different energetic starting point. These new choices will be more likely to lead her down a path of finding what she is truly looking for, because she has addressed the underlying need to heal from within herself, which is at the heart of the matter. Only then, will she have addressed the root of the problem.

I wish I could share each and every experience I have had teaching my classes. Every part of every experience has been and continues to be amazing. Those present in the classes have had the opportunity to witness many jaw-dropping miracles. Spirit always delivers. If there is a need, Spirit is there to facilitate what is necessary. Spirit consistently demonstrates the higher vibration of being in service.

Bringing It Forward

If someone's phobia is eliminated instantly and permanently by the remembrance of an event from the past, it seems to make logical sense that that event must have happened.

—Dr. Edith Fiore

My healing journey has led me to search for themes or energies I have experienced before and have brought forward into this life. I was curious to understand why I agreed to lose Elizabeth. Why would my soul want to experience such pain?

I first dabbled in past-life regression (PLR) by listening to a guided CD. A typical PLR experience begins with relaxing the body and mind and answering questions that a facilitator poses while you remain in this state of relaxation. I find PLR experiences very similar to meditation, but I am more *with it* because I have to participate by answering questions.

At first, PLR revealed the various superficial issues that were affecting me. Nine years later, when I was ready, PLR revealed the deeper ones.

In past lives, I had experienced several losses of loved ones, losses which had led me to give up on life altogether. In one PLR, I am an Indian woman. I have lost my baby in utero and never move out of my grief. I have incredible potential to be a healer, especially for women in the tribe, yet I am consumed with my own suffering.

In another PLR, I was shown two lives. The first one occurs in London, England, around 1870. I am a girl, extremely close to my older sister who marries and leaves home. I mourn losing her. As a family, we go by horse and carriage to see her because she has had a baby. I feel I have been replaced by her baby and will never be an important part of her life again. (Every time I revisit this experience, I can feel the emotion deep inside me.) I can see this situation only from my perspective. I can't see that it is natural for a mother to give all her attention to her baby. I return home with my parents, refusing to move forward with my own life.

In the second life, I am a girl of about 10. I have a stomach tumour. (During this regression, I felt incredible pain in my stomach.) My family surround my bedside. Among them are my older brother who is my husband in this life. I have decided not to get better. Being sick gets me my family's attention and devotion. They will never leave me. It doesn't matter that by leaving them, I leave them grief stricken. All I care about is that I should not lose any of them.

In this life, I have dealt with my own stomach issues. If I am stressed, I usually have some stomach pain. Growing up, I wasn't rewarded for being sick; no one fussed over me. Instead, my being sick was met with a lot of huffing and puffing. Those around me made it clear that I was creating an inconvenience for them. They would banish me to my bedroom. My husband was the first to show concern for my health. When I was sick, he would give me attention. And later, my daughters corralled around me when I was suffering. The PLR made me question whether I could be manifesting this pain for attention. When I realized that my pain was an attention-seeking device, it went away. I don't have stomach pain anymore. This is the healing that PLR can do.

I know that I have experienced many losses of loved ones in different ways, including being a deceased loved one myself. These past lives have provided experiences for my soul. In this lifetime, I am moving through my grief and participating in life again, thereby helping others in the process. This time, I have placed a pressure upon myself to "get it" right, so I don't have to do it again.

Once, during a PLR, I channelled The Council. A being from The Council stood beside me as I glanced down at the Earth. I experienced a glimpse of my life in Spirit before this incarnation. I asked, "Why do I have to go?" I usually look for ways to avoid discomfort.

The answer came swift and clear, "To face your fears."

I felt the truth of that statement deep down in my being. Yes, I am afraid of losing those close to me, whether by death or separation. But isn't that a universal fear? It is for most people, especially for those who haven't worked through their fear. So here I am, facing the discomfort of living without my daughter in the physical. It is important for me to grieve this loss, however, I have learnt that this is a limited view of what is occurring. She has shown me that she continues to be with me and is still alive. If I choose to incorporate this reality into my life, I can no longer grieve. To do so, what negate the truth of what has been shown to me: that she is alive and well.

In a Life Between Lives (the time spent in the Spirit world before the next incarnation) session, I saw myself leaving the Earth. I could see many strings behind me as they were connected to the Earth. They hindered my ability to move forward. These were energetic threads of unresolved issues. At the same time, I could feel intense pain: Pain in my shoulders (taking on responsibility); pressure on my chest (putting pressure on myself); pain across my upper back (feelings of being unloved); and pain in both arms, especially my left arm. I wanted to cut my arm off, it hurt that much. The message was to *cut if off* and let it go. I learnt that these feelings of pain are held deep within my body, perhaps even within my DNA. It is a process to completely resolve these regrets, responsibilities, and feelings of unworthiness. Understanding that I hold on to them is the first step in healing.

Destiny's Child

I slept and dreamt that life was joy. I awoke and saw that life was service. I acted and behold, service was joy.
—Rabindranath Tagore

As I put the finishing touches on this book, I had a dream. A bear is outside my door. I rush to the door and try to lock it. I look down and see that the security lock is broken. I look up and see a small brass handle that, when turned, fits into a latch bolted into a one-inch frame. I quickly turn the handle and lock the door. As the bear leans on the door, the wood starts splintering. My tiny lock is no match for the bear's strength. The bear starts entering the house. I can't keep it out. This dream tells me that I'm trying to delay my destiny. Eventually my destiny will come crashing into my life. I cannot stop it. There is comfort in knowing that what is meant to be will be.

There is so much to tell about the path to opening up to Spirit. There is so much information to share. Over the years, I've learnt a lot by teaching my classes. What I love is that Spirit has given me so many experiences to share with others as a way of teaching. Through my work, I see others blossom. Some go on to be teachers, to give readings, or to become healers. Almost everyone has been healed in some way.

As I continue my relationship with Spirit, each day is better than the last. Whenever I doubt myself, I think of all I have received and know that there is a higher purpose to my life. And as to *why me?* Because part of my life's purpose is to face challenges that will lead me to find my self-worth and to face my fears. Now that I am in my fifth decade, I realize that all my past hardships were preparation for the present. I can now bless all people and situations. I understand all is for the growth of my soul. There are no accidents. Life is not random. There is divine timing in everything. Whenever I forget these simple truths, I remind myself that there are others in Spirit who know me better than I know myself at this point in time. They have faith in me. Their love is unconditional. So, to honour our connection, I push on; I listen to my heart and find the strength that has taken a lifetime to recognize.

If I had to surmise why I am here in this life, I would have to say that it is to heal myself and, in doing so, to help others to heal. I hope my story has given you either confirmation of your own spiritual experiences or given you hope of what is possible. I am not special; nor am I different. You have the same potential to develop your spiritual gifts as I do. Why not start now? Don't leave this world with unopened gifts. Spirit only needs a crack to work with. The light can find its way through the tiniest opening. Why not open up to your loved ones and spirit helpers? They are already there, waiting to bring unexplainable richness to your life. I can't imagine living any other way. Indeed, it is our natural state to be One.

Mother

First Place Winner 2003
The Caledon Library's
Elizabeth Scavetta Memorial Teen Short-Story Contest
by Elizabeth Louise Scavetta, Age 17

I t was one of those winters. Those winters where the defiant wind blew right through you, like it knew all your secrets. The trees shivered in the cold, amused, daring you to fight back. Their bony figures rocked in the wind, taking it while they could, until they'd admit that it was the wind that was the strongest. After a life of peaceful struggle, their weakened forms would kneel before their master and collapse into the snow, dreaming of the endless slumber that awaited them. Just looking outside, you could feel their icy branches, like arms, wrap around your skin, protecting you from the storm that was coming.

My mother got up from the window seat. The blue cushion, thick as a memory, inflated with the absence of her weight. She walked into the kitchen and selected a carton of milk from the fridge. She glanced around the room, taking in the sight of unopened mail on the counter and the smell of buttered toast. Finally, she settled at the kitchen table, in front of yesterday's newspaper. She sipped her tea and listened to the gusts of wind blowing past the windows and through the porch. She looked so peaceful. Quiet, but entirely content. I smiled at her, and then she looked at me.

"It's gonna be a cold one today," she said, looking out the window now. Her velvet voice soothed my spirits. I loved Saturday mornings in December for reasons like this. We'd sit, warm and comfortable, eating our breakfasts and staring out at the snow. I would look at the trees, cradling families of snowflakes in their arms. I wondered if they envied us, warm in our pyjamas and housecoats, on the other side of the glass. *I* thought they did.

"It's a good day for staying inside, sitting in front of the fire," my mother continued. "What do you think? I'd like to read my book; actually, it's getting really good." She smiled playfully, and proceeded to describe the last passage she'd read, her bright eyes animated with delight. "Here, come on, I'll read to you." She jumped up from her chair, excitedly, and pulled me to the couch. I laughed, jumping on the living room sofa, and then snuggled in next to her. I closed my eyes against her warm, fuzzy sweater and waited for the sound of her voice.

She read to me. In a rich, melodic tone, she recounted the story, giving beauty and meaning to every line. And I listened. We laughed together, sharing the characters' joy, and then fretted during the plights. We stayed there on the couch, feeling every word as if we were in the pages ourselves. I kept listening, my head resting on her shoulder, until my mother had reached the very last page. After reading the last line, her hypnotic voice still dripping with enchantment, she gently closed the book shut.

"I love when there are happy endings," I sighed, pleased at how the story had finished off.

"So do I," my mother agreed.

"There can always be a happy ending," she continued. "But sometimes it's up to you." I nodded dreamily and gave her a hug.

She stroked my hair and kissed the top of my head. Then I curled up on the couch contentedly and fell asleep.

When I awoke, I didn't know how much time had gone by. I opened my eyes and stretched. I sat up slowly and looked around the room. My mother was no longer beside me. I stood up from the sofa and, noticing it had grown cold, wrapped the blanket around my shoulders. The grey wintry sky had not since given way to sun, and the glowing light from the fire had gone out. The walls, formerly reflecting a golden sheen, now appeared lifeless—a cheerless ashen.

I walked into the kitchen and called out to my mother. She didn't answer me. I called again but heard nothing. I stood there in the kitchen for a while, wondering where she had gone. A crow called sharply from outside the window, startling me, but there was no other sound.

I walked down the hallway, thinking that she might be in her room, and saw that her door was closed. I quietly opened the door, careful not to disturb her, but realized upon entering that she wasn't there. I stood in the doorway, staring at her vacant reading chair. The faded green chenille appeared lonely, clinging to the woollen blanket laying overtop. The room was dark, as if it had been so for years. A musty smell of bed linens invaded my nostrils, defeating the familiar scent of sweet perfume. Confused, I glanced at her desk. A layer of dust covered the top, disguising the wooden detail and yellowed papers rested collectively in the centre, immobile.

"What are you doing?"

I turned quickly to the sound of the voice, the blanket falling from my shoulders. I looked out the doorway. Patrick.

"What are you doing?" he repeated, sounding quieter this time, although apprehensive. I stared at him, not knowing how to respond. I wiped an unnoticed tear that had fallen on my cheek and turned away from him.

"Thinking about her?" he asked softly. I stood in silence for a while, not hearing him. The wind blew strong against the window, and the cold, wood floor chilled my feet. I could see the frozen trees outside the window, the snowflakes hugging tightly in the wind.

"She was here again, you know," I said after a while, distantly, still standing in the middle of the room. Patrick looked at me, and then at the floor, not knowing what to say. "I keep seeing her," I continued, gazing out the window. "She was here again. She was right there, it was so real." I could feel tears well up in my eyes. "I just miss her so much … I don't know what to do." I brought my hands to my face, covering my eyes from the truth I didn't want to see.

"I know you miss her," Patrick finally replied gently. He walked up to me and put his arms around shoulders. "But it's going to be okay," he said.

I nodded, but my tears didn't subside. We stood in that room for a while, just standing there. I was so grateful to him at that moment, but I couldn't find the words to tell him so. I couldn't shake the guilt I had for putting him through all this. My illusions of my mother were undoubtedly just as hard for him as they were for me. I hoped he understood that I was sorry.

We had not spoken of my mother much since her death two years ago. I kept trying to push her out of my mind, but the more I tried to forget her, the more I saw her. I didn't want to talk about her then, but now I felt it was time to. I wanted to talk about her; I needed to.

Patrick and I left her bedroom and sat together on the living room sofa in front of the warm glow of the fire. I told him stories about her, and we spoke for a long time, sharing our memories of joy and solace. I missed her so much. I guess that feeling never really goes away. Yet, I still believed in a happy ending.

After that, I saw her less and less. My vivid imaginings of her went from a weekly occurrence to a few times a month to nonexistent. But I never stopped loving her or thinking about her. I never totally let go of her. Someone who had taught me, inspired me, and loved me like she did would be in my heart forever. She was my heroine. Yet, I finally learned the acceptance I needed to go on. I learned it from her. She told me there could always be a happy ending. It was simply up to me.

Now when I look outside at the bright winter sky, the snow covered ground, and the trees cradling snowflakes in their arms, I think of her. I think of how she cradled me, at the kitchen table, on a December morning, in the warm glow of our home. I can think of how I've recovered the peace I had known in those days. Those days I spent with my mother.

Heather's Prayer

The following is a prayer that I use to start my meditations and when I begin to work with Spirit. You may wish to use this prayer as your invocation or use a prayer that has special meaning for you.

> Almighty God
> In Whom I lay my trust
> Fill me with your light
> Surround me with your love.
> I ask that you send your
> Angels of protection to
> Watch over me and to
> Protect this process.
> I invite my loved ones,
> My spirit helpers and guides,
> Ascended masters
> And those beings of the
> Highest love and light to
> Be with me now
> To help me with my
> Healing, understanding, and growth.
> I pray that the highest and best
> Be served for all involved.
> Thank you.

School of Miracles Dictionary of Symbols

Colours

White	Highest form of energy, includes all colours
Gold	Power, strength
Yellow	Wisdom, intellect
Green	Growth
Blue	In need of healing, concern, ongoing illness
Pink	Love
Brown	Grounded
Violet	Person is a healer, can give healing
Red	Energy, pain, passion

Geometric Forms

Upper triangle	Toward a higher source
Lower triangle	Toward a lower source
Star of David	Upper/lower energies balanced, Jewish
Cross	Jesus, coming from a high source, Christian
Crescent	New moon, spiritual rebirth, Islam
Five-point star	High source of spiritual guidance, Christian
Pyramid	Energy, power, spiritual knowledge
Circle	Completion
Sphere	Completion, source of highest energy
Wheel	Forward movement
Square/Rectangle	Block, limitation
Infinity	Never-ending, Reiki symbol

Movement

Upward	Elevation to higher state
Downward	Caution, being pulled down, moving to lower levels
To the right	Past
To the left	Future
Distant	In far future
Close	Soon/now
Driving	Present, progression
Rear-view mirror	Looking toward the past
Running	Progression, running from something
Walking	Slower progression, with caution
Windshield	Looking through toward the future

Nature

Sunlight	Energy, breakthrough
Darkness	Unaware
Mountain peak	Spiritual summit, highest point of development
Path	Moving along correct road/direction, path of spiritual development
River	Advancement, movement, strength, force, flow of life
Waterfall	Cleansing, letting go
Spring water	Spiritual cleansing, purification, purity
Calm lake/sea	Peace, calm, serenity
Stormy sea	Danger, fury, uncontrolled power, turbulent time
Fire	Purifying energy or transmuting energy
Rainbow	Harmony

Sun on water	Power, reflected energy
Forest	Rejuvenation

Objects

Oil	Calming effect, spiritual initiation
Candlelight	Direction to follow, lighting the way
Drink	Nourishment
Food	Nourishment
Temple	Place of worship, sacred vessel, coming from high spiritual place
Boat, car, plane, train	Movement from one place to another, progression (notice speed of vehicle)
Walls	Obstruction, block, protection of self, fear
Tunnel/pipe	Forward progression
Tower	Information from a high source
Ladder	Progress
Tree	Stability, strength
Flower	Growth, development
Grass	Growth, length of grass = progress

Animals

Bird	Freedom
Lion	Leader, power, strength, courage
Tiger	Striking out on your own, patience
Elephant	Gentle strength
Baby eagle flying	Progress starting
Snake	Healer, shedding one's skin
Dove	Ascension, peace
Dog	Friendship, loyalty
Cat	Care and attention

Human Forms
Baby   New beginning, potential growth
Baby in womb   A new future developing
Adult   Fully developed, in prime of life
Old person   Wisdom, maturity, knowledge

Body Parts
Two eyes   Sight, understanding
One eye   Clairvoyance, third eye
Right hand   Giving
Left hand   Receiving
Head aura   Spirituality, holiness, saintliness

ET Visions
Star formation   Reference to other worlds (planets)
Spaceships   Space travel, humans from other worlds
Space outfit   Human cosmonauts from other worlds

Spiritual
Outstretched hands Help being given by a guide/person
Outstretched arms   Great love and comfort from a higher entity

Resources

Audio Guided Meditation
Heather Scavetta, *The Swing*, 2010 Mastered by Bruce Ley Music,
www.schoolofmiracles.ca

Audio Meditation Music
Robert Haig Coxon, *The Silent Path*, www.roberthaigcoxon.com

Contest
Elizabeth Scavetta Memorial Teen Short-Story Contest, Ages 13–18,
www.caledonlibrary.on.ca

Reading
Steven A. Farmer, *Animal Spirit Guides*, Hay House,
www.hayhouse.com

Foundation for Inner Peace, *A Course in Miracles*, www.acim.org
Glenda Green, *Love Without End*, Spiritus Publishing,
www.lovewithoutend.com

J. J. Hurtak, *The Book of Knowledge: The Keys of Enoch*,
The Academy for Future Science, www.futurescience.org

Michel Newton, *Journey of Souls,* Llewellyn Worldwide, www.newtoninstitute.org

Schools
Arthur Findlay College, Stansted, England, www.arthurfindlaycollege.org

School of Miracles, Caledon, Ontario, Canada
www.schoolofmiracles.ca

Index

mutual consent in, 82
questions asked during, 81
clicks, as Spirit communication, 70–71, 106
clock image, as field of reference for Spirit relationships, 71–72
clothes, of Elizabeth, 41–42
colours, as symbols, 22, 26, 30, 123
communication. See meditation; mediums and mediumship; psychic images
control, 43, 78
core essence, 82
The Council
author's channeling of, 82, 83–84
messages from, 84–87, 108–9, 113
cross, image of, 54–55
crucifixion, vision of, 55–56
Cupid (cat), 45

D
death
acceptance of, 109
stories about, 13–14
as transition, 7, 41, 82
déjà vu, episodes of, 6
destiny, 115
development circles
author's experiences with, 57, 64–69, 101, 102–3
as therapy, 36
dictionary, of symbols, 22–23, 104, 123–24
dinnertime rituals, 23

DNA, changes in, 103
dogs, 46–49, 75
doubt, overcoming, 105, 106
drawing, by Cassandra, 51
dreams
about moving on, 59–60
delaying destiny, 115
Elizabeth's presence in, 31–32
emergency, nightmare about, 1
Palma's gift, 91–92

E
Edward, John, 14, 19
ego, 66, 68
emotions, in Spirit connection, 103
end-of-life care/issues, 90–91, 94–95
energy
blending of, 77–78
channeling of, 58
feeling/perception of, 22
loving, 80–81
lower/negative, 96–100
in pyramid energy room, 74
escape, symbolism of, 20
expectations, letting go of, 78

F
fairies, 27
faith, leaps of, 17, 40, 79
fear, 99–100, 113
feeling
of energy, 22
vs. seeing pictures, 29–30, 62
flowers, as symbols, 27, 104
forgiveness, of self, 62

Heather Scavetta, RN Non-Practising is a Reiki Master and founder of School of Miracles. She has been teaching meditation,

 psychic development, mediumship and Reiki since 2006. She has been channeling The Council since 2009. Heather developed her clairvoyant abilities after the death of her daughter Elizabeth in 2004. In her studio in Caledon, Ontario, Canada, she continues to help people who have experienced loss and those seeking more in life to develop their spiritual gifts and open up to communicating with Spirit. She and her husband, Tony, have twin girls, and live on their hobby farm with Canadian and Icelandic horses and two German shepherds.

CPSIA information can be obtained at www.ICGtesting.com
Printed in the USA
LVOW01s1305150814

399188LV00004B/7/P